S0-BHZ-900

ECUMENICAL EXPERIENCES

ECUMENICAL EXPERIENCES

Edited by

LUIS V. ROMEU

THE NEWMAN PRESS
WESTMINSTER · MARYLAND

This translation of Diálogos de la Cristiandad
(*Ediciones Sígueme*) *was made by various hands*
(*see individual essays*) *and was edited by*

LANCELOT C. SHEPPARD

PRINTED IN GREAT BRITAIN

TO

Don José Vaquero
and the
John XXIII Ecumenical Centre
of the Pontifical University of Salamanca

INTRODUCTION

Probably the best way to introduce this book and to prepare the reader for it would be to relate in its entirety the story of its birth. I shall not do so here, though I must confess that the care and attention with which its authors always listened to my requests made a great impression on me; this is borne out by the copious correspondence, and the long conversations that we held during the second session of the Council, either in the streets or at their residences in Rome. They were always very frank and cordial. It is difficult to forget those long friendly meetings with Professor Oscar Cullmann at the Valdo Centre in Rome, the perceptive and fascinating conversation of Pastor Lukas Vischer; the plans that I discussed with Fr Congar, and Hans Küng; the welcome message from our eastern brethren, represented by the Russian Orthodox observers, led by Archpriest Borovoy who, using a kind of esperanto, managed to put into words what we all felt in our hearts; Fr Terterian of the Armenian Orthodox Church, who has now been made a bishop, and many others.

In short, I wish merely to introduce you to those who, by their ready assistance, have made this book possible. What they have to say is of great interest, for they bring to life a dimension of Christianity that is largely unrealized and sometimes tragic in its implications.

Seek only in this book the aspirations of hearts that accept Christ as their Lord and God and, as pioneers of the ecumenical movement, desire to enter into it more fully and bring it to the notice of their brethren.

Illusions, hopes, desires are interspersed with autobiographical facts and expositions of doctrine, always illuminated with the light of sincerity, forming a symposium, a sort of future, prefigured unity of the Church of Christ which can already be glimpsed upon the horizon at the present time.

May I once again express my thanks for their contribution and affectionately dedicate the book especially to them. They deserve our gratitude.

Although the papers which make up this book were all written before the third session of the Vatican Council and, therefore, before promulgation of the decree on Ecumenism, they are printed here without alteration as their bearing on the ecumenical movement is unaffected.

CONTRIBUTORS

Hamilcar S. Alivisatos

Professor Hamilcar S. Alivisatos was born at Luxuri in Greece. He studied at Athens, Leipzig and Berlin. He is now professor at Athens University, President of the Greek Red Cross and an active member of the World Council of Churches.

What motives led you to take an active part in the ecumenical movement and what do you expect from it in our time?

This question, as put to me by the editor of this book, at a time when the ecumenical movement in one form or another seems to be prevailing in the whole Christian world, is of very great importance, because it challenges both my personal position and attitude and that of my own (Greek Orthodox) Church towards the movement. Yet the answer to this rather complicated question is not so very difficult because, practically speaking, it depends on what the ecumenical movement really is.

If it is true, as I believe it to be, that the ecumenical movement is in essence nothing but recognition of the evil of separation in the Christian family and the expression of the will to annihilate this evil for the accomplishment of our Lord's fervent wish "that all may be one" (John 18. 20), then the motive of every true Christian in taking an active part in the ecumenical movement is very evident.

The ecumenical movement, begun by such convinced Christians, came into existence through them and through the initiative of some of the Protestant Churches; they accepted the idea and, more or less officially, have put into action the effort of the understanding of all the Christian Churches, as to the value and the necessity of their union. It is this effort which brought about the co-operation of several Churches (including the Orthodox Church) for the formation of the World Council of Churches which, so to speak, officially represents the ecumenical movement. This common task of the co-operating Churches aims at the future union of all Christian Churches and, through this, the restoration of the once united Church as desired by Christ and envisaged by St Paul in his letter to the Ephesians.

This effort of the World Council of Churches finds expression (1) in very important and serious welfare work among the Christians of the world, and this is an expresssion of Christian love among needy Christians and non-Christians; and (2) in a thorough investigation of the existing differences between the Churches and in the theological preparation of a kind of status as to their relations, which would be something similar to the standard of union once expressed by Vincent of Lérins: *In necessariis unitas, in dubiis libertas, in omnibus autem caritas.* If such a status is officially accepted and agreed upon by the co-operating Churches, it will be the first step towards the real union and reconstruction of the one and undivided Church.

The agreement to such a scheme for co-operation will mean the restoration of unity among the separated Churches, that is, of the real Body of Christ. It is worth while mentioning on this point that the Orthodox Church first took the initiative of proposing to the other Christian Churches the organization of a kind of co-operation and intercommunion in the field of Christian love, long before the formation of the World Council of Churches.

Soon after the First World War the Ecumenical Patriarchate of Constantinople, after 400 years of barbarian pressure, feeling itself in a somewhat easier position, in 1920 issued its famous encyclical to all Christian Churches urging them to form a kind of "League of Churches" in accordance with the example set by the then newly formed "League of Nations".

This initiative of the very weak Orthodox Church was a result of its fervent and continuous prayer "for the peace of the whole world, the good standing of the holy Churches of God and the union of all"; it was due, also, to the bitter experience of World War I, and the anxiety of the impending danger of World War II, which later followed.

Soon after the Orthodox Church found itself in even worse condition than before, owing to the great disaster in Asia Minor in 1922 and also because of its great struggle in Russia under Marxist Communism. On account of this, the Orthodox Church was unable to pursue its original suggestion.

Thus the initiative passed to the Protestant Churches, already busy with a similar movement through the separate organizations of "Faith and Order", "Life and Work", and "World Alliance for promoting international friendship through the Churches" which were finally amalgamated in the "World Council of Churches".

The Orthodox Church has co-operated with the Protestant Churches and has become an active member of the World Council of Churches in spite of conditions far worse than ever before in its existence.

Lately, when the great movement was in some way adopted (but in another form) by the Roman Catholic Church through the initiative of the great Pope John XXIII and his Second Vatican Council which undoubtedly inaugurated a new period of Church history, the Orthodox Church without any hesitation suggested to the Pope the opening of a theological dialogue between the two older Christian Churches to arrive at an understanding for the final annihilation of the great schism of the ninth and the eleventh centuries. This dialogue has already begun with the historical meeting of the Pope of Rome, Paul VI, and the Ecumenical Patriarch of Constantinople, Athenagoras, which took place in Jerusalem.

The great hope is that this anticipated deeper understanding of the two Churches will work on parallel lines with those already in existence with the World Council of Churches. A good omen for this appears to be the invitation of observers to the Vatican Council from all Christian Churches, showing the new attitude of the Roman Catholic Church towards the ecumenical movement; and this, of course, without any danger of disturbing in any way the basic principles of her unchangeable doctrines and Church order.

Thus the second reason why I am active in the ecumenical movement is the endorsement, so to speak, by my own Church, of which I am a faithful member, of my personal attitude towards, and faith in, the reconstruction of the one holy catholic and apostolic Church.

To these two reasons a third may be added. In our days, two world-wide idealisms are struggling against each other: the strongly united front of materialism and, facing it, the terribly divided Christian theory of life. It is the struggle between the spirit of this world and the Children of Light, similarly described in St John's Revelation. Will the Children of Light lessen their spiritual power by the continuation of their sinful separation?

These are the motives which led me to take an active part in the ecumenical movement (and it may be of interest to the reader to know that I am the oldest living member in the ecumenical movement); and the result I expect from it in our time is nothing else but that soon, very soon, all real Christian individuals, and through them all Christian Churches, will wholeheartedly endorse what St Paul says in his Letter to the Philippians:

> If anything is meant by encouragement in Christ, by loving sympathy, by common fellowship in the spirit, by feelings of tenderness and pity, fill up my cup of happiness by thinking with the same mind, cherishing the same bond of charity, soul knit to soul in a common unity of thought. You must never act in a spirit of factiousness, or of ambition; each of you must have the humility to think others better men than himself, and study the welfare of others, not his own. Yours is to be the same mind

which Christ Jesus shewed. His nature is, from the first, divine, and yet he did not see, in the rank of Godhead, a prize to be coveted; he dispossessed himself, and took the nature of a slave, fashioned in the likeness of men, and presenting himself to us in human form; and then he lowered his own dignity, accepted an obedience which brought him to death, death on a cross. That is why God has raised him to such a height, given him that name which is greater than any other name; so that everything in heaven and on earth and under the earth must bend the knee before the name of Jesus, and every tongue must confess Jesus Christ as the Lord, dwelling in the glory of God the Father (Phil. 2. 1–11).

Jean-François Arrighi

Mgr Jean-François Arrighi was born at Vico (Corsica) in 1918. He studied in Marseilles, at the Institut Catholique in Paris and at the Sorbonne. He is under-secretary of the Secretariat for Christian Unity (Western section) and a member of the Congregation for the Eastern Church.

THE SOURCE OF MY ECUMENICAL VOCATION

I have had since my childhood what might be called the vocation to enter in close relations with what was not the traditional Catholicism of the Latin rite. I was brought up, and I still spend my holidays, in a Corsican village called Cargese which had been founded by Peloponnesian Greek refugees from the yoke of Turkish rule. There were two churches in this little village, one Greek and one Latin, and this taught me from my early youth that Catholicism was not identical with the Latin rite and the western forms of Catholic Christianity. Then came my secondary schooling in France, where, coming in contact with Protestant schoolfellows, I was struck by their strong Christian faith and great knowledge of the Bible. Among my own family I was also in contact with fine people who devotedly lived an authentic Christianity as members of the French Reformed Church. All these things, it is clear to me today, were a good preparation for taking part in an ecumenical movement.

My Studies for the Priesthood

It was from my time at the Sorbonne among many fellow students who belonged to the JEC (*Jeunesse étudiante chrétienne*) that I became concerned about the problem of the unity of the Churches. The influence which I must mention in particular was that of Father Congar's *Divided Christendom*, for it was after reading this book with much thought that I gave myself seriously to the elucidation of means by which reunion might be sought. Such lecturers at the Catholic Institute in Paris as Fr Daniélou, S.J., Fr Henri, S.J., and the Oratorian Fr Bouyer in their courses were constantly endeavouring to open their students' minds to ecumenical considerations. At this time I was busy spreading the writings of Abbé Couturier, and I knew two men in particular who at that period and often in the midst of difficulties were working as forerunners in a field which was as yet little explored. One was the unforgettable Dom Lambert Beauduin, founder of the Union monastery at Amay (later at Chevetogne); the other the Archimandrite Christopher Dumont, O.P., founder of the centre of studies "Istina" in Paris. We observed the annual Week of Prayer for Christian Unity in the chapel of the University Seminary of Paris where I was studying, and of this I have one special memory. It was during that week in January 1945, and a new Nuncio had just arrived from Rome, Mgr Angelo Roncalli. He presided at solemn Vespers on the Sunday, and after Fr Bouyer's sermon he himself spoke to us. This was the first time that I had heard an official personage of the Church give direct encouragement to work for union and ecumenical labours. There were many occasions after this when I was able to hear the Nuncio, in his sermons or in private conversation, express his ideas on problems of reunion and ecumenism. I could not but be encouraged by all these experiences along my path of investigation into means of achieving unity.

Work at Rome

When I arrived in Rome to complete my studies for the priesthood, I made the acquaintance forthwith of the *Unitas* circle which had been founded by Fr Boyer, S.J. He too had been a forerunner, devoting himself to the diffusion of the ecumenical spirit in Italy with the help of some other priests, secular and regular, nearly all of whom were foreigners. Thus it was that over a period of ten years I traversed Italy from north to south preaching either during Christian Unity Week or on days devoted to ecumenical education, especially in the seminaries.

During the years when I was at the Sacred Congregation for the Eastern Church I worked under Cardinal Tisserant, who before the Secretariat for Christian Unity existed always warmly welcomed those of our separated brethren who paid a visit to the Eternal City.

I was then, too, in contact with Mgr Willebrands, the secretary of the Catholic Committee on Ecumenical Questions. He often came to Rome and we enjoyed some long and far-reaching discussions. Eventually I was called to work much more closely with him in the Secretariat for Christian Unity.

During all the years, then, which preceded my taking a place in this Secretariat I had been in contact with a whole world of ecumenical concerns and activities, and nearly all of us who had been chiefly concerned met again in the organization brought into being by John XXIII with Cardinal Bea as president. Henceforth, then, there will be this organization in Rome to which our separated brethren may address themselves. The ecumenical voices no longer belong to private individuals; it is the Church herself who takes part in the dialogue. For myself, I can only give thanks to God for having called me to unite my labours to so great a work.

[This contribution was translated by Rachel Attwater.]

Gregory Baum, O.S.A.

Father Gregory Baum, O.S.A., is in charge of the Centre of Ecumenical Studies in Toronto. He was born in 1923 in Berlin of Jewish parents and became a Catholic in 1946. He entered the Augustinian Order in 1947 and studied for the priesthood at Fribourg in Switzerland. He is a Consultor of the Secretariat for Christian Unity and a *peritus* at the Council.

THE CATHOLIC APPROACH TO CHRISTIAN UNITY

There was a time when we thought of Christian unity simply in terms of conversions to the Catholic Church. The efforts of those concerned with the reunion of Christians in the one fold of Christ were directed to one single aim: to make as many converts as possible among Protestant Christians. This attitude was even reflected in our prayers. Praying for Christian unity as we did, and still do, during the Unity Octave simply meant asking God to give grace and light to Protestant Christians so that they might discover their errors and return to the Catholic Church. If we read the "intentions" which were attached to the different days of the Octave, we find in them a perfect expression of this attitude to Christian unity.

While, as Catholics, we still believe and always will believe that the Roman Catholic Church is the unique community of Jesus Christ, our approach to Christian unity has undergone a great change. What exactly has happened? I wish to describe this change in the following pages.

First of all, we have begun to look at our separated brethren more dispassionately. We have examined their teachings and their ways of life more carefully and made the startling discovery that much that is Christian and supernatural is alive among them. This is true especially of the older and more traditional Protestant Churches. Taking for granted their good faith, we must conclude that many elements which have come into this world through the Gospel of Jesus Christ have retained their vitality among Protestants. We are often impressed by their spirit of faith, the firmness of their hope, and the amplitude of their charity. Among them we often find prayer, sacrifice, a deep appreciation of sacramental baptism, and a love for the breaking of the bread described in the Gospel. It is true, we also find other elements among Protestants, scepticism and unbelief, a disregard of the faith of the New Testament Church, doubts about the divinity of our Lord Jesus Christ. But, then, we also know many Catholics who do not go to church, who do not live a life of faith, and who yet support the "Catholic" side in social or political conflicts. One thing we know—that salvation and holiness will come to Protestant Christians if they follow what is authentically Christian in their denominational traditions. More than that, we believe that Protestant Christians who, with supernatural charity, are faithful to Jesus Christ and his call move along a road which brings them closer to the fullness of the Gospel as it is taught, or should be taught, in the Catholic Church. We must be very careful not to offend Protestant Christians by our way of speaking about them; for by offending them we could impede their progress on the road which leads them closer to that Christian fullness which is also the ideal of the Catholic Church. Being unappreciative of their Christian spirituality and continually stressing their need of "conversion" must offend Protestant Christians and thus render a disservice to Christian unity.

There is a second factor which has contributed to the change in our approach to Christian unity: we have begun to take seriously Protestant criticism of ourselves. I do not mean that we should pay attention to the voices of bigotry and prejudice which still exist in the Protestant world, or rather, to use a phrase of a famous Protestant author, in the Protestant underworld. But we should take very seriously the intelligent and thoughtful criticism offered by Protestant leaders, especially by their great theologians. We certainly are in need of criticism. We can never relax with the feeling that we have reached the perfection which Christ has laid down for the Church. While we believe that the Catholic Church has received the fullness of Christ's gifts, we also believe that we are sinners, that we have not lived up to this fullness, that we have often presented a one-sided picture of the Gospel, have overemphasized certain aspects of divine truth and neglected others. For this reason, then, we can learn from the criticism of Protestants.

Let me give two simple examples. If we read in the best of Protestant writers that the Catholic Church has given a place in religion to the Blessed Virgin which is out of proportion to her place in the Gospel, we acknowledge that this accusation brings to light a deep divergence between the Protestant and the Catholic understanding of divine revelation. At the same time we must recognize with humility that there are certain popular devotions and prayers to Mary which obscure the full Catholic teaching on Mary's dependence on her divine Son. Can we not learn from Protestant criticism to speak about Mary in such a way that nothing of the Church's christological teaching is forgotten? How many Catholics know that Jesus still prays for us? According to Catholic teaching, Jesus is not only our God who grants us new life, but also our brother who intercedes for us before his Father in heaven. Or, when we read that Protestants are afraid of Christian unity of the Catholic type because they dread centralization and the lack of freedom granted to local Churches, can we not admit that the present centralization of the Catholic Church is not a dogmatic necessity but an accident of history? The present centralization is not essential to the Church's divine structure, nor does the supreme jurisdiction and the infallible teaching of the Pope imply that he is the only legislator or the only authentic teacher in the Church. At the Second Vatican Council a multitude of Catholic bishops advocated a decentralization of ecclesiastical government. The supreme power of the Pope will in no way be slighted when the bishops of the Church regain the awareness and practice of their collegiality, and episcopal conferences of various countries receive freedom to adapt their Churches to the needs of their people.

These are just two examples of how we can profit from Protestant criticism. There are many others. We must learn to listen to the Spirit speaking to us through criticism of others!

These considerations lead us to a third factor which has produced a change in our approach to Christian unity. Being aware, on the one hand, of the Christian values alive among Protestants and, on the other, of the possibility of learning from their critical remarks, we come to the conclusion, painful though it may be, that we, too, must change. This sentence must be understood correctly. The Catholic Church cannot change in her divine structure: we cannot change our teaching or our sacraments: but, since the divine structure of the Church is cast in a human and historical form, there are large areas of Catholic life where changes are possible, normal, and necessary. In the above paragraph I have suggested some of these "changes", a more christological way of venerating our Lady and a greater share in the government of the Church on the part of bishops. There are many others that could be named. The Vatican Council has suggested many areas where change is possible and necessary.

The urgent demands of Pope John XXIII and Pope Paul VI that the life of the Church be adapted to the needs of the modern world was their great contribution to the movement for Christian unity. The Pope as well as many Fathers of the Council are well aware that many barriers which prevent others from understanding the true nature of the Church are barriers which we ourselves have erected. It is up to us, therefore, to take these barriers down. And if the Vatican Council should reform the Church in this way, then not only Protestants will gain a deeper insight into the nature of the

Church, but we also will understand more profoundly what Christ wants to do in and with his Church.

Apart from the great changes that can only be initiated by the Catholic hierarchy, there are other smaller, yet still significant changes in Catholic life that are up to our priests and the laity. For the sake of Christian unity, we all can make our spiritual life more biblical and more liturgical. We can try always to put the emphasis on what is central in our Catholic faith, on our redemption in Jesus Christ, and understand the other elements of our faith from their relationships to this central mystery. Our moral life must spring from our incorporation in Christ, not simply from a submission to a set of laws. Our devotions must be fed from our access to the One Mediator, not simply from a seeking of personal blessings. The words of our creeds must be sources of life for us, not formulas passively accepted. This is the way of the New Testament and this is the way of the Catholic liturgy.

Summing up, then, there are three factors which have altered our attitude towards Christian unity in recent years: the appreciation of the authentically Christian among Protestants, a serious consideration of their criticisms, and the willingness on our part to renew and reform the ways of Catholic life. Much more then can be done in favour of Christian unity than persuading a few Protestants to become Catholics. While we have no right to disparage individual conversions to the Church, we feel that our first duty in regard to Christian unity is to change ourselves. We must discover to what extent the image of the Church which we create really manifests her true nature and to what extent it deforms it: and then have the humility to change, to improve, to grow spiritually.

For this reason it is quite inadequate to suggest that the aim of the movement for Christian unity is "the return of the separated brethren to the true Church". If we speak of the return of the others, we suggest that we have nothing to do but wait for them, while the great insight of the ecumenical movement is that we, too, must be willing to undergo transformation. We certainly believe that God wants to reconcile all Christians in the Catholic Church, but we also know that at the time of such a reconciliation the Catholic Church would have to look very different from what she does at present. Seeking Christian unity is not a return to something, but a going ahead towards greater fidelity to Christ.

With this "new" attitude in the heart even the prayer for unity which we offer during the Unity Octave takes on a different quality. Praying for the unity of Christians we do not simply ask God that Protestants may discover their error and come closer to us; we ask with an even greater intensity that we may discover our own shortcomings and that the Church receive the grace to be reformed. That Christians are disunited is a terrible sin before God, but why should we in our prayers point an accusing finger at others? Should we not rather admit that we, too, are responsible for Christian divisions, not only in the past but even in the present, whenever our pride creates an obstacle to the unity that Christ desires for his people. Only if we are humble will God hear our prayer *that all may be one.*

Charles Boyer, S.J.

Father Charles Boyer, S.J., was born in France in 1884 and was ordained in 1916. He is Professor of Theology at the Gregorian University in Rome, President of the international association *Unitas* and editor of the review of the same name (it appears in English, Italian, French and Spanish). He is a member of the Secretariat for Christian Unity.

AN ECUMENICAL TESTIMONY

I am answering briefly, and most willingly, the two questions which have been asked me: why did I involve myself in the ecumenical movement and what hopes do I place in that movement today?

I was born in a little Catholic town which preserves a memory of the religious wars. Above one of the ancient gates of the town, the visitor is shown an outer stair from which one of the great stones is missing because a girl dropped it on the head of the Huguenot commander. This story or legend, which did not inspire ecumenical sentiments, testified to the division of Christians. The priests at Saint-Sulpice taught me to pray for the conversion of England. When I entered the Society of Jesus I learnt as a matter of family history all about Catholic apostolic activities with regard to the Churches of the Reformation and to the Eastern Church. Teaching theology made me penetrate into the very heart of the controversies. I had, however, no thought at all of direct action. But one day I was invited to sit on a committee which was being formed with a view to promoting Christian union. I then became interested in the ecumenical movement: the *Unitas* society came into being and, in 1948, I found myself sufficiently well prepared to profit by the kindness of M. Visser 't Hooft and to be present at fairly close quarters, though only as an onlooker, at the birth of the World Council of Churches at Amsterdam.

It is undoubtedly the existence of the ecumenical movement which gives a special attraction to the work for unity by opening up new vistas of hope. I think we must go back as far as Newman in order to understand what we are seeing today. With the Tractarians, one of the Churches separated from Rome since the Reformation had questioned itself about its own legitimacy and its situation in relation to Rome. Tentative efforts in the direction of union had continued in England and had produced encouraging responses from the great Pope Leo XIII and, at the dawn of this century, the desire for unity had sprung up in many places and in many souls. Working to re-create Christian unity has become one of the tasks imposed on our day and age. By amplifying and accelerating the ecumenical movement, Pope John XXIII revealed himself as the instrument of the Holy Ghost.

The disaster brought about by these divisions is immense. If Christians had remained united we should not see two-thirds of the human race outside the pale of Christianity. The progress of secularism and neo-paganism would have been more effectively checked. Whatever people may say, the channels of supernatural life have silted up in many Christian communities, not always to the same extent, but always to a very considerable one. It is not without great detriment that the disciples of Christ have lost the unity which Christ asked for those who were to believe in him, and their testimony in favour of the Mission of the Son of God sent to save us has weakened in consequence. The remedying of such a disaster, even if he can only make a very small contribution to it, is one of the noblest aims a Catholic priest can set before himself.

What hope can one reasonably entertain of the re-establishment of unity? In one sense it is boundless, for God is all-powerful and he loves mankind. Nevertheless, the difficulties that confront us today are such that, judging them by the normal course of events, we must distinguish various possibilities according to the greater or less distance which separates the different confessions from the Catholic faith. For—and we must keep this clear in our minds—a Catholic cannot admit that unity can be realized before Catholic dogmas and Catholic morality have been accepted by all Christians. Our Orthodox brothers are not separated from us by a very wide ditch, said Leo XIII ("non ingenti discrimine seiunguntur", *Praeclara gratulationis*). Their attachment to the great mysteries of the Faith, their eucharistic liturgy, their belief in the infallibility of the Church, their veneration for the Mother of God and for the saints, as well as the attitude of their best theologians and the radical changes in political conditions, all inspire me with the confidence that the end of the schism is no longer very far away.

The sons of the Reformation do not constitute a single solid block. The majority of them maintain a conscious and only too real separatist attitude towards the Catholic Church. Nevertheless, it does seem that fairly numerous groups which one sees being formed in various countries and which have turned towards Rome might accept the whole Catholic faith. For the others, at the present moment, we can do nothing but long, work and pray.

But the final aim of ecumenism presupposes intermediate ends which are valuable in themselves and which already justify ecumenical activity. In the first place, there is the new climate which has been created and which can be improved still more. Indeed, the last and most typical characteristic of ecumenism is that, instead of looking first and foremost at the differences which separate the Christian confessions from each other, we are forcing ourselves to recognize and to appreciate justly what unites them. The disruption took place in the distant past. Those who today belong to the Orthodox Church or to the Christian bodies which owe their origin to the Reformation did not cause the separation; they received it as a heritage, as a result of being born into a milieu which had been cut off from Rome for centuries.

Their wish is simply to be Christians in the traditional way taught them. They themselves are deeply distressed by the disunion they observe and they strive to restore unity. Therefore it is expedient to make what we have in common our starting-point, to see its importance, to consider its exigencies and to reach out together towards a wider and wider understanding. From now on, we treat each other as brothers; we respect each other, we help each other, we love each other. Conversation between us is therefore possible and everything permits us to believe that it will be fruitful.

Catholics willingly admit that, in making contact with their brothers of other Christian denominations, they themselves have also much to gain, not only because the exercise of charity makes for holiness, but also because conversation forces one to see one's own position better and to distinguish more clearly between essentials and inessentials. It also leads us to profit by the felicitous way in which another communion has developed some particular point of doctrine or a particular Christian practice. Christians drawn closer together among themselves will be able, from now on, to collaborate in order to promote their common interests. All those who claim Christ as their Lord can work together for the defence of the religious idea, for social progress, for everything that conduces to the preservation of peace and the elevation of mankind.

I think I have answered the questions I have had the honour to have had put to me, and may I have made ecumenism loved as I see it myself, in the light of Catholic principles.

[This contribution was translated by Antonia White.]

Pedro Cantero Cuadrado, Archbishop of Zaragoza

The Most Rev. Pedro Cantero Cuadrado is a Doctor of Philosophy and Theology of Comillas University and Doctor of Civil Law of Madrid University. He became bishop of Barbastro in 1951, of Huelva in 1953, and (since writing this essay) Archbishop of Zaragoza in 1964. He is a member of the Secretariat for Christian Unity.

SPAIN AND THE ECUMENICAL MOVEMENT

The present ecumenical movement originated as a sociological fact in the missionary field, and more especially among the Protestant missions. It was, and still is, in the work and atmosphere of the missions that the echo of "Unum sint" acquires greater and more pressing pastoral significance and that the reality and existence of Christian unity must be seen and felt more fully, "that the world may believe that thou hast sent me" (John 17. 21).

From reasons and circumstances such as these it follows logically that the christianizing sensibility of the ecumenical spirit should be more in evidence and more developed in nations where the people live in an atmosphere of religious plurality, where the divisions among the believers and Christian communities constitute a problem for the spreading of the Gospel itself. If ecumenism in its spiritual dimension is directed towards drawing together all Christians in Christian unity, its urgency is to be seen and felt more poignantly among those nations where the division of Christian brethren is a more pressing and painful reality quantitatively and qualitatively.

Against the background of these mental and missionary realities and perspectives it is not difficult to understand that Spain's attitude towards the ecumenical movement is endowed with special characteristics. Spain is a country of Catholic unity, not only from the demographic point of view, but also from a far deeper point of view, namely, the religious spirit of the Spanish people, who, since the existence of Spain as an independent nation, have known no other than the Catholic, Apostolic, Roman religion, either historically or sociologically.

Nevertheless, it is precisely on account of this profound Catholic spirit in its life and its history that the nature of Spain and Spaniards is eminently ecumenical, a knight errant of the unity of the whole human and Christian family. Spain's evangelistic work in the New World, in Africa and in the Philippines is a living testimony of her ecumenical attitude. No differences of race, colour, class or culture prevented the Spaniards from intermarrying with the inhabitants of the regions evangelized by Spain, because according to the Catholic faith of Spain "there is neither Greek nor Jew, circumcision nor uncircumcision, Barbarian, Scythian, bond nor free, but Christ is all, and in all" (Col. 3. 2).

Spain, faithful to the Catholic Church, realizes now, together with the Popes, the Second Vatican Council and all Christendom, that ecumenism is a spiritual movement in the service of Christian unity; and Catholic Spain is taking part in this undertaking with all the wealth of wisdom and experience of its Catholic and ecumenical spirit. If in all parts of the world the ecumenical movement demands a certain climate, mentality and spirit, also—and perhaps with more reason—in Spain it must influence the ways of thinking, feeling, loving and behaving of Spanish Catholics towards their "separated" brethren, and *vice versa*, the latter's behaviour towards Spanish Catholics, within a universal, human and Christian perspective, of the common good of the Spanish nation, and of the universal common good of the Catholic Church and the international community.

It is to this end that I believe Spanish Catholic ecumenical centres should direct their co-ordinated prayers and efforts.

[This contribution was translated by A. F. Price.]

François Charrière, Bishop of Lausanne, Geneva and Fribourg

The Right Rev. François Charrière was ordained priest in 1917 and became bishop of Lausanne, Geneva and Fribourg in 1945. He is a member of the Secretariat for Christian Unity and was the official representative of the Roman Catholic Church at the jubilee celebrations of Patriarch Alexis in Moscow.

You have asked what were the motives which led me personally to take an active part in the ecumenical movement. I shall give my answer quite simply and directly.

Although I was born in Switzerland, a country of which the majority of the population are Protestant, I was not anxious about the problem until I came in contact with non-Christian students who had travelled to Europe for higher studies. Among the Chinese in particular I was struck by the scandal which Christian divisions and antagonisms presented. Christianity is a spent stream, they said, its flow has almost ceased; it is now forming a delta and soon will be lost in the sea.

It forms a delta—the metaphor impressed me profoundly, and I have never forgotten it. Until that time I had lived with our divisions. A curate at Lausanne more than forty years ago, I was in daily proximity to Protestants who at that time constituted three-quarters of the citizens. We had the best of relations with them at the civic and temporal level but from neither side did we ever, or hardly ever, touch on religious questions. I busied myself with the faithful of my own parish, prayed that God would enlighten and sustain all men of good will, and was so used to our divisions that the effect they might have on non-Christians hardly occurred to me. From the moment when I had evidence of the degree to which our dissensions were a stumbling-block to those who were not members of the Christian family, I began to take an active interest in all things which might help to bring together Catholics and Protestants, but not forgetting, of course, Catholics and Eastern Christians. After I had written a number of articles on this grave and delicate matter, Bishop Besson, my revered predecessor, asked me to join a study conference which would include representatives of the Protestant and Orthodox Churches and of the Catholic Church. For many years I have taken part in meetings which have enabled me to come into contact with distinguished figures of the ecumenical movement centred at Geneva.

So it was that concern for the apostolate among non-Christian students led me to seek close relations through prayer and study with our brethren at our side, non-Roman Christians. I had not first thought of those who were so near, but of those much further from us, and it was their reactions in the face of our divisions and disagreements which caused me to confront the scandal of divided Christians.

You have also asked me what are my expectations of the ecumenical movement today.

I am speaking with many others when I say that we cannot look for immediate, spectacular results. That coming together and ultimate reconciliation which form our aim and our prayer will be a work of time, as the Popes have so frequently reminded us. Any attempts to hurry the movement would have precisely the opposite results. If there was ever a field of work which demands the greatest sensitivity and patience it is this one. People's souls are not to be fashioned as one carves blocks of stone. It must never be forgotten that it is God alone who moves within them, in the keep of that fortress which is every man's personality. Those things which are hurried on, or which are attempts to force human plans before the time is ripe, can only endanger the goal or at least delay its attainment. There must be no question of humiliating or vexing, looking for victories in fact; we must rather seek in complete submission to truth and real charity the mutual reconciliation of Christians. When it happens that we are wearied because we are not seeing quick enough results from our labours, it is because we are, without realizing it, working for ourselves; we want to see that little seed, which we have ourselves sown abroad, shoot up and give fruit. It is the Lord who gives the increase; but we must beseech him without respite, through the Blessed Virgin, Mother of Jesus and of all the Christian world, for the reconciliation of Christians.

[This contribution was translated by Rachel Attwater.]

Yves M.-J. Congar, O.P.

Yves M.-J. Congar, O.P., was ordained in 1930 and is the author of many well-known books, among them *Divided Christendom, Lay People in the Church, The Mystery of the Temple,* etc. He is a *peritus* at the Second Vatican Council. One of the leading theologians at work in the Church today.

MY FIRST STEPS IN ECUMENISM

If there is one point about the ecumenical movement which gives it originality and power, it is that it owes its origin to *facts*. It represents, of course, a movement of ideas, it involves questions of doctrine, but it does not itself spring from the efforts of any thinker of genius, nor from intellectual deductions or doctrinal elaboration. Ecumenism has given rise, and will still give rise, to many studies in theology, history, etc., but these studies come to serve a spiritual movement which owes its birth and development to facts of a spiritual order, facts which we cannot doubt have God for their prime author.

The action of God is seen in this fact (which, according to theology, is the special work of the Holy Spirit), that a great many men have found themselves moved, without previous knowledge, to work in the same direction. Something inside them has led them, imperatively, but without violence, from within, *suaviter et fortiter*, to devote themselves to the cause of Christian unity. When they began to work in this field they realized that a great many others had heard the same call. Without previous agreement, often without even being acquainted, these men found themselves working at the same task, even though not in the same way: that was inevitable, since they came from such different backgrounds and started from such different presuppositions.

It was in 1929 that I recognized the ecumenical call for

myself. I did not then call it that. It was simply the question of the unity of all the disciples of Christ; but I was thinking chiefly of the Protestants, whom I knew best. I was already pondering questions of ecclesiology, for in the summer of 1928 I had chosen as the subject for my lectorate thesis, "The Unity of the Church". I was to be ordained priest on 25 July 1930, and was fervently preparing for that great interior change. To that end I was studying not only the theology of the eucharistic sacrifice and the priesthood (for which I benefited greatly from Canon Masure's book, *The Christian Sacrifice*), but also the Gospel of St John, chiefly with the help of the commentaries of St Thomas Aquinas and Fr Lagrange. It was while studying the seventeenth chapter of St John that I recognized in myself a call to work for the unity of Christians. I at once told my superiors, and I must say that they have never offered the slightest opposition or objection, even when they were not convinced that my activities were of much use.

After my ordination I often celebrated the Mass "for the unity of the Church in time of schism", as it is called in the Dominican Missal. There again I met John 17, and taking my stand on the idea (theologically well grounded) that the priest at the altar is himself a sacramental reality, at least in the wider sense of the word, I used to read the Gospel as it were *in nomine*, even *in persona Christi*; I would re-enact that unique Prayer, in the power of which our own prayer has all its being, rather in the way that our consecrations (in the Mass) draw their efficacy from the first, and in a sense unique, consecration of the Bread and Wine in the Upper Room. Generally speaking, my theological work has always been closely bound up with liturgical celebrations. I owe a great deal of what I have grasped in theology to these celebrations. The liturgy is truly inspired in the manner in which it uses and brings together the scriptural texts of which it is woven. Thus it conveys a very deep sense of the mysteries which it celebrates. My celebration of the Votive Mass for Unity played a part in my theology of Unity and Ecumenism. It is not for nothing that my book *Divided Christendom* ends with the Alleluia verse for that Mass in the Dominican Missal:

Aedificans Jerusalem DOMINUS,
Dispersiones Israelis CONGREGABIT.

I soon set to work, at least as far as my continually heavy occupations allowed. I learned German, and in Germany I found some annual numbers of the review *Hochkirche*, which, in spite of certain questionable positions, gave me a certain documentation and a breath of enthusiasm. In 1932, being free to enjoy some months of personal, uncommitted study, I attended some lectures at the Faculty of Protestant Theology in Paris. There I formed friendships, some of which have proved remarkably lasting.

I was teaching apologetics, and in this field I had read a vast literature. I need not emphasize what it lacks: in books, in the absence of anyone to answer you, you triumphantly refute all your opponents. In reality, that is not how things happen. Moreover, whenever you personally and directly study a thought, or a point of history, you find that things are not exactly as you had been told. I have often found this to be the case, especially with Luther, whom I know something about. But this depends on study: it is valuable, indeed very important, but it is not enough. It is absolutely necessary to meet the men themselves; one must have experience of the Others, one must hear them explain themselves and their convictions, one must see them praying, meet the concrete reality of their religious life. And so in our study, even scientific study, of the Others, we have advanced from "Symbolics", which studied only texts and doctrines, to *Konfessionskunde*, or the Phenomenology of the Christian denominations, which in principle adds to the study of doctrines that of the forms of life, of worship, of social formations, etc. But what is the use of purely academic study of a religion, compared with direct experience? I confess that I have learned more from direct contact with Protestant, Orthodox and Anglican friends than from books. Or at least, I have understood the books, to a great extent, by means of the contact. I have understood more about Anglicanism by being present at Evensong, or Compline in a college, than by reading their dogmatic books, which we sometimes find rather disappointing. But the fact is that for either, the essential is not to accumulate information but to come face to face with something *genuine*. Professor Lortz once said to me, on the subject of Grisar's *Luther* (better, however, than Denifle's): "There is no book with less falsehood about Luther, and no book with less of Luther himself." The same could be said of many Catholic publications on the East and Orthodoxy. They are very valuable on the level of information and documentation, and often in sheer erudition; if, for example, you want to know whether Photius did this or that on 3 April or 30 March. These facts are valuable on their own level. But if we want to *understand* Photius or Orthodoxy, we must go beyond them. One can learn more of these subjects by assisting intelligently at some Eastern liturgies and by friendly conversation with some Orthodox Christians.

I think that one of the marks of a true vocation is keenness to know what has been done already in one's chosen field, and an interest in the pioneers. The study of the classics, indispensable for all true culture, responds to a similar need. I should have grave doubts of the theological vocation of anyone who did not eagerly read St Augustine and St Thomas Aquinas. Personally I felt drawn to the men who had done or tried to do something in the field of Christian divisions and unity, and especially to a humble French priest, Fr Fernand Portal, a Vincentian, who from 1895 onwards had not only worked for *rapprochement* with the Anglican Church, but had inspired many priests and laymen to serve the sacred cause of unity. I had not known him personally, nor had I ever seen Cardinal Mercier, but I had read everything to do with their activity and the Malines Conversations. I was able to approach only some of the survivors of these (M. Hemmer on the Catholic side; on the Anglican,

Dr Kidd; when I visited that most sincere and humble man at Keble College, Oxford, he asked me for my blessing—me, his inferior in both age and learning!). At York Minster I venerated the ring which the dying Cardinal Mercier had taken from his finger to give to his friend Lord Halifax.

But several of the pioneers or forerunners were still alive. In 1932 I visted Dom Lambert Beauduin, then in exile near Paris. In the same year I made my first visit to the monastery he had founded at the behest of the Holy See, which is now at Chevetogne, but was then at Amay (Belgium). Dom Beauduin's ambitions have now been more than realized. But before he died he had the joy of seeing not only the beginning of the pontificate of John XXIII, whom he had known well, but the promulgation of the Council, for which he had longed. His work survives, as living as ever, and as one reads those early works (1925–6), one finds that they are still valid.

It was at Amay in July–August of 1932 that I first met Abbé Paul Couturier. It was only later, when I read his life by Fr Maurice Villain, that I learned how that visit of the Abbé to Amay had marked a turning-point in his life, for his dedication to what was his vocation, his grace, and to a great extent his work, the Week of Prayer for Unity, from the 18 to 25 of January.

The Week (or, as it was more often called, the Octave) of Prayer for Unity had existed since 1907, or at least since 1909. Catholics had adopted it, though it was Anglican in origin (Paul Wattson in the United States, Spencer Jones in England), but they kept it by allotting fixed days for the conversion of the Protestants, the Anglicans, the Jews, etc., as well as lapsed Catholics. It was all too clear that on these conditions neither Protestants nor Anglicans could associate themselves with us in our prayer. The wording of the intentions had indeed been altered in an interesting way: prayers would be for the sanctification of the Protestants, the Anglicans, etc. That was better, but it still meant praying that the Others might become better. By successive approaches, and in such a way that his basic idea was outlined in his mind in 1935, Abbé Paul Couturier (who as a Benedictine Oblate had taken the name of Irenaeus) modified the Week of Prayer so as to refashion it. His formula, which will no doubt be explained elsewhere in this collection, is well known: to pray for the coming of that unity which God wills, by the means which he wills. Thus the Protestants and others could join us in our prayer: thus, once a year at least, we could ensure that our prayer would be unanimous, simultaneous, converging. And in fact, having preached the Universal Week of Prayer for unity every year since 1936, all over France and the adjoining countries, I can bear witness that I have seen the peaceful victory achieved by this prayer. It is a great time of grace. I always return from it exhausted, but a little more converted to the Gospel. I have seen the Week win over towns where it was unknown. I have seen attendances doubled, increased tenfold. I have experienced, almost physically, an extraordinary quality of attention: so profound and religious that the like can only be found in the services of Holy Week and the Easter Vigil. Conference flows spontaneously into prayer. God is present.

It was Abbé Couturier's vocation to give ecumenism its heart of prayer and love, and to this vocation he was heroically faithful. He used to prolong the Memento at his Mass, praying by name for all the heads of Churches, all the workers for unity, all the causes which concerned it. With no secretariat, he carried on an immense correspondence, which was a kind of sacrament of his presence, besides the writing and despatching of his tracts, in which he made known his thought and his mystique.

My way was clearly the way of prayer, but more specially it was the way of theological work: the doctrinal service of the People of God. It is a difficult way, and a way in which one may often be wearied and hurt. Since 1932 I had taken part in a certain number of ecumenical gatherings, and I shall say in a moment how profitable they were to me. In January 1936 I was invited to preach the "Octave of Prayers" for Unity at the church of the Sacred Heart in Paris. I gave a series of conferences, fairly elaborate and carefully constructed. The editing of these in the following months resulted in a book, *Chrétiens Désunis* (English translation, *Divided Christendom*, London, 1939), which inaugurated, in 1937, a new series devoted to ecclesiology, called *Unam Sanctam*. In this present year I am going to contribute the fiftieth volume of this series, a collection of studies which I shall call *Chrétiens en dialogue: Contributions catholiques à l'Œcumenisme.* Its title recalls the earlier one, but the differences are significant of certain changes which have taken place since 1937. The divided Christians are now in dialogue. As the Holy Father said in Bethlehem on the Epiphany, 1964, they can now no longer evade the question of their unity. Moreover, it is now no longer Catholic ecumenism we are dealing with, but the Catholic contribution to ecumenism, which has an original, though relative, unity. It derives this from the very unity of God and his Holy Spirit, who has begun, in the world of our divisions, a work of good neighbourliness, of *rapprochement* and convergence, towards a point of concord and unity.

Then and ever since, in many encounters, sometimes purely private, sometimes corporate and almost official, I have had the unforgettable experience of what ecumenism brings to anyone who devotes himself to it, always presuming the indispensable conditions of seriousness, preparation, assured Catholic loyalty and, finally, realism and common sense. Ecumenism has given me much, so much indeed, and of things which have so worked in my innermost life, that I can scarcely tell the tale of them.

Every contact with Another who is really such obliges us, in the first place, to be what we profess to be, for our good. One is, as it were, driven to be what one professed to be, but was not really. Man needs to be confronted with something else: if he faces only himself, or what is similar, either he becomes insipid, or he invents artificial tensions. Ecumenism has broadened me, it has "de-provincialized" me, without breaking my attachment to my roots. It has made me know other Christian men, in whom there was clearly something of great worth. I have striven to see realized a state of theological thought and of Christianity in which this "worth" of the Others should be integrated and lived in communion or unity. Ecumenism appeared to me, from the outset, as a work of integral Catholicity. But, by thus giving me elements of *plenitude*, it drove me to seek for *purity*: two things which seem difficult to harmonize, for some look for plenitude at the expense of purity (the Catholic temptation), while others are haunted by purity at the expense of plenitude (the Protestant temptation). Ecumenism provides elements in the sense of plenitude, but at the same time it demands a great effort of purity, for we are faced with great difficulties. By this confrontation I am obliged to leave behind the easy assurances of a slothful orthodoxy, of a certain spirit of triumph, in order to find, not insecurity, which has no claim to be an ideal, but truth which is renewed from the sources, criticized, and acquitted of the accusations which used to be levelled at our positions. In this necessary research I remake my theology, my soul and mind alike draw from it an expansion and at the same time a unity, which give me great joy. Ecumenism shows me and gives me an unknown half, as it were, of my self. It makes me, not less Catholic, but more genuinely Catholic. If I could become perfectly a Catholic, what Christian could refuse to become my brother?

I would add that the problem of the encounter with the modern world is, *positis ponendis*, very similar to the ecumenical problem, at least as to the intellectual *data* of the problem and the attitudes of mind. At bottom, Christian divisions and the world which was born of the intellectual and political revolution together form part of that History which we are required to assume in a Christian manner. All that is part of our task, for which the grace of God will not fail us. As for our Christian divisions, we are called to assume them in penitence and hope: ecumenical penitence and hope.

[This contribution was translated by P. J. Hepburne-Scott.]

Oscar Cullmann

Professor Oscar Cullmann's work is known throughout the world. He is one of the leading Protestant theologians and is Professor at the Universities of Basle and Paris.

For more than thirty years I have taken part in the ecumenical movement; it was a necessary consequence of the intellectual fellowship that I felt with Catholic biblical scholars, and more especially New Testament scholars. For this reason I regarded the ecumenical work undertaken at Geneva as insufficient; at the beginning, at least, it only envisaged the union of the non-Roman Christian Churches. Of course, I have no desire to criticize the efforts, and the magnificent results, of the organization at Geneva. That was the only way for them to begin. Yet living in daily contact with Roman Catholics I considered that a Catholic-Protestant dialogue was especially urgent and, observing that there was a very real intellectual fellowship between the Scripture scholars of the two communions, it seemed to me that in the field of biblical studies, of great importance for us all, the dialogue could be particularly fruitful. For this reason I sought all the opportunities possible for exchanges of this nature.

This was at a time when there were still very few contacts between the theologians of the two Churches. I remember particularly, too, a conversation that I had with Fr Congar when I was a younger professor at the University of Strasbourg between the two wars. Afterwards, I was in close touch with Fr Braun, O.P., the New Testament scholar, at that time Professor at Fribourg in Switzerland, now Court Chaplain in Brussels. I was astonished how our views agreed in exegesis. My friendship with Fr Braun brought me face to face once more with the problem of the scandal of our separation. I saw that particularly it is on the question of the primacy of Peter that we are divided and that, on a last analysis, the impossibility of forming one single Church can be ascribed to our differing conception of unity.

While I was doing the preparatory work for my book on St Peter I visited Rome for the first time; the Waldensian theological faculty there had invited me to give a course. It was on this occasion that I made the acquaintance of Cardinal Tisserant, who discussed biblical questions with me and obtained for me an audience with Pius XII. The latter gave me permission to inspect the excavations beneath St Peter's; I devoted an important chapter of my book to them. Pius XII told me during the audience that he was in favour of a "dialogue" in every way possible between exegetes of the two Churches. The desire expressed in the Preface of my book *Peter: Disciple, Apostle, Martyr* that an entirely candid discussion should take place on the subject of the primacy was fully realized after the publication of my book; I am pleased indeed at the spirit in which the discussion took place.

During this first visit of mine to Rome I made the acquaintance of several eminent Catholic theologians. They did not come to my lectures at the Waldensian theological school—they were forbidden to do so—but I was invited to give a public lecture at the faculty of letters in the University of Rome; the crowded audience was made up, for the most part, of Catholic theologians. They had read my books and were anxious to make my acquaintance. Thus I received many invitations from them and was struck by their openness of mind. It is impossible for me to name them all, but I ought to give a special mention here to three Institutions which subsequently largely contributed to a deepening of my relations with Catholic theologians. In the first place I must mention the Biblical Institute. There I came to know Fr (now Cardinal) Bea, who was then rector of this remarkable Institute. I remember that he showed me the Encyclical *Divino afflante Spiritu* which had only just been published; it is a document of immense importance for biblical studies and was hailed at the time as a real act of liberation by Catholic Scripture scholars. I recall the important conversation I then had with the Rector and how impressed I was with his personality. Since then I have met him very frequently. Every year I go back to the Biblical Institute and I feel myself at home there. I am friendly with most of the professors there, and particularly with Fr Lyonnet.

At the same time professors at the Gregorian University welcomed me; another house to which I go back with pleasure year after year is the Benedictine monastery of S. Anselmo on the Aventine. The late Fr Mohlberg, together with my colleague Eric Peterson, invited me there for the first time. Nowadays at the monastery table, to which I am invited yearly, the Abbot (Benno Gut whom I had already met at Einsiedeln) and the rector, Aug. Mayer, are friends of mine.

Whereas during my visit to Rome, about fifteen years ago, there was hardly any contact between the Waldensian Church and Catholic theologians and no Catholic, as I mentioned above, was present at my lectures, I was pleased to observe that my yearly presence in Rome helped to break the ice and that year by year the number of Catholics in my audience has increased and that even high dignitaries of the Roman Church have been present in recent years at my lectures.

Other very fruitful contacts between Catholic theologians and myself have grown up at the Sorbonne in Paris, where my regular courses of lectures have become real ecumenical meetings between Protestant and Catholic students. I have had Catholic students who have become famous—Dr Hans Küng, professor at Tübingen, Fr Lanne, O.S.B., rector of the Greek seminary in Rome, and others as well. Even Fr de Lubac, S. J., has been present at one of my lectures at the Sorbonne (École des Hautes-Études). It is a special joy to me every fortnight to see in my audience Protestant students in theology sitting side by side with Catholic students, all following together in the Greek text the interpretation given by me of the New Testament as I occupy what used to be the chair of A. Loisy and M. Gaguel. I was especially moved on the occasion of my sixtieth birthday when, before I began my lecture, a Protestant theological student and a Catholic student belonging to the Franciscan Order (he is now a professor) offered me their good wishes and made me a presentation in the name of all the students.

In Paris also I have frequent contacts with leading theologians, with my colleagues at the École des Hautes-Études, Frs Festugière and de Menasce, Abbés Roques and Nantin, and above all with Fr Daniélou of the Institut Catholique. The friendly debate that I had with the last named on "Scripture and Tradition" was very fruitful and his objections were of great assistance to me in clarifying my own position, and indeed in correcting it on certain points. Nor must I forget my relations with the Dominican priory at Le Saulchoir where I had the great pleasure of meeting for the first time my eminent colleague Fr Spicq, the Scripture scholar; in the exegesis of the New Testament I feel my position to be very near his own. At the present time I am glad to say he is my colleague at Fribourg in Switzerland. He came to the celebrations for my sixtieth birthday at the University of Basle and with Fr Strassmann spoke of the community of ideas between us in explaining the New Testament.

In German-speaking Switzerland my dialogue with Catholic theologians was initiated by conversations with Hans Ur von Balthasar. At a later date I had discussions with Otto Karrer . . . I could mention many others. All have confirmed me in my profound conviction that while we are separated at the ecclesiastical level, we are not "separated brethren" but brothers in Christ.

I shall not mention the extraordinary ecumenical experience that presence at the Vatican Council has meant for me. I was invited to it as a guest in my private capacity by the Secretariat for Unity. The new relationships that I established, my sharing in what is called the Catholic Pentecost, the theological discussions with Fathers of the Council, have all been for me a confirmation of the enduring truth that Christ unites us despite the division of our Churches. Yet I cannot pass over in silence the profound impression made on me during the first session by the late and much lamented John XXIII whom, by the good offices of Cardinal Bea, I was enabled to meet before the Council. Nor must I omit to mention the evening that I spent at the Vatican, towards the end of the first session, alone with the present Pope, at that time Cardinal Montini, and the frank and cordial discussion that we had. In memory of it, as I was leaving, he gave me a bronze crucifix which serves as a perpetual reminder to me that we are already united by the cross of Christ.

I attach particular weight to the positive result of all these encounters because I have always been careful *not to conceal what continues to separate us* and to emphasize especially those points which, in my view, constitute insurmountable obstacles to a union at the ecclesiastical level; this leads me to speak of a question on which I have set my heart.

Formerly it was theology which separated us, nowadays it draws us to union. I have the foregoing account of my ecumenical experiences to prove this. Yet I believe that at the present moment the problem is rather the following: how are we to extend to the laity the change of climate that has occurred among the theologians of the two Churches? How are we to introduce the ordinary laity, among whom there is still considerable mutual misunderstanding and distrust, to the positive results of our dialogue, and especially to the fundamental result which is the conviction that we are united in Christ?

The week of prayer which owes so much to the late Abbé Couturier is one of the means of doing so. But I have sought, in addition, to make use of a *visible* means, the only one that is practicable at the present moment. It did not come to me merely by human means; it occurred to me through the Bible, the New Testament, through the thought of the first

Council of all—the council of the Apostles. I refer, of course, to the ecumenical collection for the poor of Jerusalem, which nowadays can only be the mutual offering of Catholics and Protestants made during the week of prayer. My plan is put into practice every year in many places throughout the world. Unfortunately, it has not been understood by all. But I am profoundly convinced that ultimately it will win acceptance and that the twenty-first Ecumenical Council will help to make this practice, decided upon by the Apostles at the first Council, very general. I am convinced of it because I am sure that it is the will of Christ and I shall not let myself be discouraged by any setback or lack of interest which my proposal may encounter in the future. Once there is in existence a means of making the union of all Christians *visible*, ought we not to do everything that we can to carry it into practice?

[This contribution was translated by Lancelot C. Sheppard.]

George Florovsky

George Florovsky is a well-known Russian theologian. He was born in Odessa and belongs to the Russian Orthodox Church in the U.S.A. A specialist in patristic studies, he is at present Dean of the Seminary of Wladimir in New York and a professor at the Union Theological Seminary of Columbia University. He is a member of the central committee of the World Council of Churches.

THE ECUMENICAL DIALOGUE

In 1926 the late Nicolas Berdyaev invited me to join in the ecumenical conversations he started at that time in Paris. The group included representatives of several Churches: Eastern Orthodox, Roman Catholic, and Protestant. Various basic questions, mainly of a theological and philosophical nature, were taken up and discussed. Discussion was usually on a high level. The most active participants in the discussion were Jacques Maritain, Gabriel Marcel, Marc Boegner, Winifred Monod, Sergius Bulgakov, to name but a few. Occasionally Père Lebreton, Etienne Gilson, Edouard Leroy would also take part in the conversation. It was at once an encounter and a confrontation. The confrontation was often rather sharp and heated, but always in the spirit of mutual respect and confidence. It was my first ecumenical experience. These meetings taught me to appreciate the value and the potential of ecumenical dialogue, across the boundaries of denominational and cultural commitments. These meetings continued for two years. Then a smaller group, including Catholics and Orthodox only, continued to meet privately in the house of Berdyaev for some years.

My second ecumenical experience was of another character. It was connected with the Fellowship of St Alban and St Sergius, in England. The Fellowship began, in the late 20's, under the auspices of the British Student Christian

Movement, as a small and informal group. It consisted mainly of students in the Universities and Theological Colleges, with a number of senior advisers, of which the most outstanding were in the early period Bishops Charles Gore and Walter Frere, of the Church of England, and Father Sergius Bulgakov, of the Orthodox Theological Institute in Paris. The first aim and purpose of the organization was to bring together younger members of the two Churches, Anglican and Orthodox, for mutual acquaintance and joint discussion of various problems of common concern. A number of members of other Churches were in attendance from the very beginning. With the course of time it became usual to have some Roman Catholic guests present, of whom may be mentioned the two Benedictines, Dom Bede Winslow, of St Augustine's Abbey, Ramsgate, and Dom Clement Lialine, of Amay and Chevetogne, in Belgium. Special emphasis was put on the exchange of devotional experiences. The participation in the work of the Fellowship provided ample opportunity to observe the life of the Anglican Communion, both on the parish level and on the level of theological research and training. It was again a kind of dialogue and confrontation, informal and unofficial, an exchange of views and problems, a sharing of experiences.

Both of these early ecumenical involvements of mine were of informal character. By the nature of the case there is no room for making decisions. It was a great advantage that the dialogue could be free and intimate, one could be sincere and outspoken. We could meet each other in complete Christian freedom. This did not exclude controversy, but even the controversy was dominated by the conviction that "divided Christians" still do "belong together" and stay under the mighty challenge of the call to unity. This dialogue has helped me to discover both the common ground of the universal Christian commitment and the depth of actual estrangement and tension. It was at this point that I was inwardly compelled to develop the sense of "ecumenical patience".

In 1937 for the first time I had occasion to participate in a larger and more official ecumenical gathering—the Second World Conference on Faith and Order, in Edinburgh. It was still primarily a dialogue and a confrontation of different traditions and communions, in search for agreement and disagreements, but this time on a wider, more comprehensive, and semi-official scale. The participants were delegates of their respective Churches, though without any authority to take decisions. Crucial questions were raised in the discussion, including the problem of ministry and sacraments. Precisely at this point the ultimate divergence was disclosed, and inevitably had to be admitted openly, that there was no chance of agreement. In my opinion, this was the greatest positive achievement of the Edinburgh Conference. The whole ecumenical problem appeared in its complexity and its paradoxical tension: the strong urge for Christian unity and the impasse of factual diversity and divergence.

It was at that time that I was called to close participation in ecumenical work, at the top level, as a member of the small Committee of Fourteen, which had been set with the task of preparing the foundation of the World Council of Churches. This Committee was then enlarged and became the "Provisional Committee of the World Council of Churches in the process of formation". It continued its work till the First Assembly of the Council in Amsterdam, 1948, when the Council was officially inaugurated. For the long period, up to the Third Assembly of the World Council in New Delhi in 1961, I was deeply involved in various forms of ecumenical activity—in study groups, in editorial committees, at the Ecumenical Institute, and indeed in large gatherings, such as Assemblies—Amsterdam, Evanston, New Delhi—and World Conferences on Faith and Order—Lund and Montreal. It was an enriching and welcome experience. My personal concern, however, was always with dialogue and confrontation. The theological discussion was properly focused on the process of ecumenical co-operation, new vistas have been discovered, and new awareness acquired. But the crucial problem remains as it has been before. The ultimate goal of the ecumenical endeavour has been more accurately formulated or articulated, the basic difficulties have been more courageously ascertained and acknowledged. And this is indeed a major achievement. On the other hand, it was becoming increasingly evident that in "divided Christendom" there was actually no real agreement concerning the basic issue—the very "nature", or true character, of that unity which Christians are bound and called to seek. It may be contended that "divided Christians" are not yet ready for the true unity, and probably are not willing or prepared to proceed. It may be suggested that the historic "Ecumenical Movement", as it had been promoted first by the endeavours of "Faith and Order" and "Life and Work" and then institutionalized in the World Council of Churches, had reached its critical peak or climax. The task is of an enormous complexity, although the promise is still great. Disagreements are manifold, inveterate, radical. And there is no room for any compromise. This must be faced frankly and courageously, without reticence or evasion, rather with confidence and trust. The actual division is profound. Short cuts and easy ways must be avoided. One has to be bold enough to meet the challenge of Christian tragedy. The inner challenge, growing up among the various constituents of the World Council, in which the Protestants and the Orthodox are paradoxically joined in common endeavour and search, has been increased by the growing impact of the "ecumenical awakening" in the Roman Catholic Church. The perspectives of ecumenical endeavour are drastically widened. One may react to this impact of "Roman Ecumenism" in various manners, with hope, with indifference, with suspicion, with apprehension, with fear. But it is difficult to ignore the challenge. The very concept of "Ecumenism" changes its character and scope.

Now, it is still possible to evade the challenge, or to

postpone the crisis. It is possible to reduce "Christian unity" to the dimensions of a "co-operation" on practical matters. It is not a new device. Already at Stockholm, in 1925, it was declared that "doctrine divides, and service unites". Indeed co-operation and solidarity in practical matters is in a sense also a contribution to Christian unity, if only to a certain limit and only in the case when the secondary or subsidiary character of such a contribution is honestly acknowledged. In fact, this "co-operation" may easily become an impediment, an obstacle, or an evasive substitute for the true search for unity. The root of disunity is much deeper than historical estrangement or mutual isolation. The root is of a religious and doctrinal character. An effective co-operation of the "divided Christians" on social issues, or in the field of "international affairs", without any deeper urge for ultimate "union" in One Church, can but obscure or even distort the vision of true "Christian Unity", which is the unity in faith and order, the unity of the Church and in the Church.

One of my basic convictions, which grew gradually out of my ecumenical experience and committed meditation on all the issues involved, is that "Ecumenism in space" which has been practised in the current endeavours is insufficient and should be supplemented by what I came to describe as "Ecumenism in time". The ecumenical experience itself has shown that encounter or confrontation of the divided Christian groups or communions, in their present state and form, cannot break through the deadlock of denominational diversity, and of all sorts of isolationist prejudices, unless the perspective is enlarged to include the whole range of Christian historical tradition. In fact, "modern" Christians have become so excessively "over-modernized" in their attitudes and orientation as to lose access to the very foundations of Christian faith and reality which came to seem "archaic" to them. One has to recover the true historical perspective, not to be paralysingly imprisoned in detached "modernity". In any case, the major task of Christians, in their existential situation today, is still in the field of theology, of "faith and order", not in the "practical" field, and, probably, not even in the "pastoral" field, if pastoral concerns are detached from "theology" or even opposed to theology. The only effective way of ecumenical "action" today is still the way of theological study, dialogue, confrontation. It is, of course, not a smooth way. Indeed, it is a stony way, strewn with terrible stumbling-blocks, which for centuries accumulated in the period when "unhappy divisions" had full sway. In my opinion, it is the right way, precisely because it is so arduous. The task is to remove the stumbling-blocks, not just to ignore or to evade them.

Moreover, is it not obvious that the great change in the ecumenical situation, and a very real change, in recent years has been brought about precisely by the devout work of dedicated theologians, even in the separated denominations? The new, more adequate and more existential understanding of the Word of God, of Holy Scripture, is the fruit of devout biblical scholarship. Church historians, in spite of their continuing disagreement on many crucial points of interpretation, have drawn for us a new picture of the "*common* history" of "*divided* Christendom". Patristic scholars have demonstrated the perennial value of the ancient Tradition, which is existentially valid and challenging now no less than in the past. Liturgiologists have quickened the understanding of devotional values, and even the historical soundings in this field have enriched the inner life of contemporary worshippers and believers. In brief, if we find ourselves now in a changed and renewed world, as we actually do, and better equipped for grasping ecumenical problems, it is due chiefly to the indefatigable labour of those who concentrated their efforts in the field of theological research and meditation. Moreover, a fruitful ecumenical co-operation has been achieved now first of all in the field of theological research, not only in the areas of technical studies, but also in the areas of intensive doctrinal interpretation. A truly ecumenical dialogue is going on with unusual impetus and energy. Indeed, one must be cautious in the evaluation of the immediate impact of this work on the total situation in the Churches. The average churchman, in all denominations, is still hardly aware both of ecumenical problems and of ecumenical progress. Again, the very growth and partial success of ecumenical comprehensiveness inevitably produces counteraction and the increase of denominational rigidity in various circles. There is, in many quarters, a tendency to eliminate, at least practically, the Eastern Orthodox from the ecumenical dialogue and to reduce this to a "Catholic-Protestant encounter", under various pretexts. On the other hand, there is an obvious anxiety, in some quarters, about Roman Catholic participation in the ecumenical dialogue. And the majority is probably simply indifferent to the ecumenical issue, in all its shapes.

Personally I am not looking forward to any spectacular events in the ecumenical field in the near future. Nor am I interested in the official negotiations concerning unity or reunion. There is much work to be done on the more intimate level and in an informal way. And this work must be done. There is an urgency and there is a promise. But the advance is in the hands of the Lord.

Jean Guitton

Jean Guitton, distinguished French philosopher, member of the *Académie française*, was chosen as the first auditor at the Council by John XXIII. He has for many years shown an active interest in ecumenism and has written several books on the subject (e.g. *The Church and the Gospel* [London, 1961]).

ECUMENICAL RECOLLECTIONS AND CONSIDERATIONS

The most important stage in my ecumenical education came in about 1925 when Father Portal introduced me to Lord Halifax. A strange character, this Vincentian, who did not seem to have the obvious qualities for the task which God was to entrust to him—spiritual leadership in a great school, work for the union of the Churches; for he was not an intellectual or a theologian, not a diplomatist or a historian, nor even a speaker of many languages. I remember, too, how this man, who knew so well how to draw others into conversation, would himself keep silent. His singular gift, which he maintained with almost peasant tenacity, was to open minds and souls to the future.

The unguessable part to be played by providence was a meeting and then a friendship which, in its springing up, personal nature, practical creativity and triumph over death, bore the character of love. The two men were of different worlds; the one a gentleman in the Victorian style, an aristocrat who knew the crowned heads of Europe, the other a very French peasant priest, reflecting still, in the tradition of Monsieur Vincent, the writings, customs and manners of the seventeenth century. Their harmony lay in their sharing a spirit at once mystical and practical, and in being young in heart, with a kind of chivalrous spirit in their service of

Christ and the ambition to do great things together, like that of Nisus and Euryalus in those lovely lines of Virgil:

Dine hunc ardorem mentibus addunt,
An sua cuique deus fit dire cupido?

"Do the gods give this fervour to our souls, or is each creating a god from his desire?" The great desire (perhaps chimerical in the form it took) was the return of separated Churches and the Anglican Church in particular into unity. It had become apparent since the Oxford Movement that God's grace was freshly at work in that Church, separated as it was from the visible body. Newman had leapt the gap in one moment of illumination. Halifax, following the tradition of Pusey, remained in his Church with the aim of prevailing upon it to cross the gulf slowly and as one body.

This is not the place to go into details of the historical episode which I am recalling; but I shall outline the lofty ideas which inspired these two forerunners.

In the first place, nothing is impossible with God the Almighty; and as Christ willed the unity of all in his name and offered his life for that end, as we read in John 17, there can be no greater work than to labour for it, whatever the obstacles.

Secondly, that as the Churches were separated bodily and through the action of their leaders, it must be by a similar movement and again under the guidance of their leaders that Christians will come together. Those in positions of responsibility, then, must meet in order to understand what unites them and what divides them, seeking to lessen the differences in a spirit of charity without damaging truth. All goes for nothing if there is refusal to meet face to face; an essential step has been taken when it becomes possible to talk together. Once the misconceptions caused by language are cleared away, the areas of agreement are found to be wide. There must be no surprise at checks or vexation at delays, but all must be taken in good humour, knowing how to wait for a long time and when to take a new step.

It is necessary, thirdly, to determine the actual methods to be involved in the union of one Church with another, as Leibniz had tried to explore. On the part of Rome there must be preparations for a period of transition, and on the part of a Church coming into union there must be concessions for the sake of consciences, going as far as the acceptance of re-ordination. It is possible to revive ancient customs and usages such as marriage of the clergy in some cases, and an effective patriarchate. It is possible, also, to envisage new patterns of ecclesiastical government. Knowledge of the past must be deepened in order to make out more clearly the as yet veiled shape of the future.

Finally, difficult, perhaps terrible, times may well be coming in the history of the world; but the ultimate significance of these conflicts, dividing nations and social groups, is to be found in the light of that union in himself for which Christ prayed to his Father.

These are grand conceptions. Mystical thought, statesmanship in the best sense of the word, intelligent apprehension of Christian history, imagination, all are there.

Thus came, perhaps a little feverishly, the anxiety to lose no chances, to try every opening, and the visits to Canterbury, the calls on the Vatican, pamphlets for publicity, meetings, times of great hope, dramatic occurrences, fortunes and misfortunes. Cardinal Mercier himself had in full measure the too uncommon gift of being able to arouse men's imaginations; always a leader rather than a negotiator, he preferred the appeal to the people to the appeal to the prince. He also sympathized deeply enough with Lord Halifax, his "dear Viscount", to state the question of unity before the world at large and its opinions, a method which has hardly been customary in the Roman Church.

If we ask when the nineteenth century came to a close, we may hesitate between the end of a way of life in 1914 or the engulfing of the old national liberties in 1940. However that may be, we speak of Father Portal's generation as one which is already part of history; their time is over and others have taken their place. Even a number of Father Portal's disciples are now dead: Abbé Morel, Antoine Martel, Maurice Legendre, and quite recently Jacques Chevalier. New signs point to a change; we have entered on another age.

The more profound idea of truth and unity has taken the place of that of separation and reunion. The word ecumenism, so ancient and yet contemporary, which raised hardly more than a doubtful smile in the nineteen-twenties, has taken on a significance not fully defined but rich. Above all, the Protestant world, which had rather held itself apart from more purely ecclesiastical controversies, has entered into the movement towards unity. The problem of union as it is met with between Churches which have preserved the episcopate, like the Orthodox and the Roman Church, is very different from that between the Reformed Churches and Rome. The first, difficult though it may be, appears solvable on a human plane, but the latter only on the divine.

There is at the same time the existence of a mixed type, like the Church of England, which in accustoming Protestants in a free atmosphere to a Catholic sense of things and, on the other hand, familiarizing Catholics with something of the Protestant religious experience, encourages the resumption of contacts broken for centuries. Discussion takes the place of controversy when each seeks not so much to show that he is right (as in the correspondence between Bossuet and Leibniz) as to meet for mutual enlightenment when each makes known his faith with the wish to relate it to that of the other. Theologians re-evaluate every question from the ecumenical viewpoint, to lessen differences in the light of the five centuries which Roman Catholics and the Reformed Churches revere in common, or to distinguish possible developments in the idea of the Church or the mystical body. Ancient forms of liturgy are revived; the Eastern liturgies are better appreciated. Certain Catholics are attracted to more ancient forms of prayer; while Protestants may rediscover the divine office, the breviary. Catholic re-estimation of the life of the laity and the married state works in the same direction, enabling them to esteem the pastoral virtues, without a confusion with the priesthood which remains in its proper high position.

When I compare modern times with the period which followed the First World War—*quindecim annos, grande spatium*—I notice in the new generation a less anxious desire for immediate results. We are no longer in the age of Leo XIII, when there was a feeling of the "last things", and the reconciliation of the French Republic with the Church, social concord, or the union of the Churches was looked for tomorrow. Leo XIII had imparted his high hopes to people at large; and these were felt among those who had grown up in his period and lived before 1914. The concept of corporate reunion hardly focused and absorbed attention until the years from 1930 to 1960. There was as it were a delay in the Parousia. In the Church of the first century, the second coming of the Saviour on the clouds of heaven, to judge the living and the dead, was expected. The Lord delayed; and there was a development on earth, the organic episcopate grew, thus fulfilling the purposes of Christ. It is rather the same here. Some people expected the return of Anglicans at an early date, in 1894 or 1921. But this was delayed, and there was a development in the world—ecumenism, through further prayer and a deepening of concepts. In this way, ecumenism could be described as the delayed return.

The following are some of the patterns of thought in philosophy, concerning the Church and the ecumenical ethos, as it appears to a Catholic mind.

Ecumenism requires reflection on the idea of truth in relation to charity. Its position is between two conceptions both of which it rejects, though not with equal force, the one being essentially false, the other seriously deficient.

The first of these is the pragmatic notion of a minimal ecumenism. In despair of full agreement, there is a search for those things which the Churches have in common, and this "lowest common multiple" becomes the pattern of the Super-Church. Or, in the manner of Hegel, differences are accepted within a more "comprehensive" truth which may be obtained by making a synthesis. Or again, it is reckoned that there are different families or branches in the Church, like the religious Orders: why should not Protestants, Russians, Anglicans form as it were three ecclesiastical bodies rather on the style of the orders of Dominicans, Franciscans and Jesuits? Other forms of this ample ecumenism may be imagined.

The remarkable thing is that this is becoming less and less accepted even in Protestant circles, and that this is related to a profound apprehension of the nature of religious truth. The religious mind, in its greatness, makes the same demands as that of mathematics. It is seeking a truth, that is to say an absolute. It is highly sensitive to exactness, and will die for an iota. Martyrs are people who could have saved their lives with a monosyllable. If there were tyrants in geometry who insisted on subscription to the proposition that "the sum of the angles of a triangle is 179 degrees", then the true mathematician could not but choose, rather, the concentration camp. Or if he was told that we are going to take an average of seven different solutions, then he would know that that answer would be false. Thus also is it in the sphere of religion: the concept of truth is the mainspring of faith.

The second of these mistaken conceptions may be called rigidity. It lies in saying: "I have the truth and you are in error. I am staying where I am; you come to me."

This is a much less extreme error than the first; that was a negation of the concept of truth, while this is only a kind of exaggeration of it. It is truth without charity. Ecumenism is precisely the overflowing of charity into truth in order to complete it.

What, then, is this uniting of charity to truth which makes it a living whole? In the first place, when one finds that as a heritage or by conversion one has the gift of truth, then the duty accompanies it of seeking to give it out again as the greatest of good things. But there is a further consideration. If we do not make the effort to see from the point of view of the other person and to share in that part of the truth which he possesses, then it is our own truth which will be found incomplete. Such a proposition might have been a little shocking in the Middle Ages because then a union of minds was realized in Christianity, and the sphere of thought was held to be co-extensive with that of faith. However, even in that period of international Catholicism, the greatest thinkers did not hesitate to face what at one time seemed their strongest enemy, the works of Aristotle, in order less to overthrow than to assimilate them. But in the age of divisions which followed the sixteenth century and in which we still live, the truths became disassociated, and the methods those of opposition. The love of truth found itself parting from charity—from the love of truths, wherever they are to be found, and the desire to grow in their knowledge.

Truth which is not imbued with the wish to share it is not a living truth; it will soon find itself involved in self-love or threatened by paralysis. We can never be quite sure beforehand what in fact is going to disturb us in others; it might be errors in faith (in which case we may be justified), or a falsity of language or attitude by which their faith, or ours either for that matter, is overshadowed, or very possibly the irrevocable nature ascribed by us (or by them) to venerable customs which are none the less inessential. We can all think of examples.

Seen from this point of view, ecumenism entails the principle that the effort of sympathy cannot come from either side alone. We are not to expect the others to do all the work; all must be prepared to expend themselves to the utmost. Paul set out on the journey to Damascus ultimately because Stephen delivered himself to be stoned in Jerusalem.

To the difficult, the hard road which non-Catholic communities or individuals have to take towards the Church, there must correspond among Catholics an equal effort, though a different one, that is to make the path of return easier, built more firmly on humanity. Newman expressed this when he said that the Church must be ready for converts as well as converts ready for the Church.

A second aspect of ecumenism is expressed by the statement that ecumenism is devoted to deepening the idea of the catholicity of the Church.

It has to be remembered always that from the Catholic standpoint the Church is not seeking a basic element which is lacking in her symmetry or essence. To be a Catholic is to believe that one has entered into the pivot of truths, known in past or future, the nucleus or the seed, the centre around which all things must finally take their position. Our separated brethren know that if we kept silent on this we should no longer be in a fit condition to talk with them, because we should have ceased to be true to ourselves. But to be a Catholic is also to see Catholicism, while perfect in its essential form, as in a state of growth until it has gathered all things into itself. To be a Catholic is to have a sense of unity, a unity expressed by the word and history of Rome; but it is also to hold that this unity will not be fully accomplished until all aspects of human diversity may find themselves at home within her, when all the varieties of human experience shall be brought into unity. It is, then, to maintain a double concern, or rather two concerns, one following on the other, and which meet in the heart. The first is that of unity— "there will be one fold, and one shepherd". The second is that of diversity which respects the individuality of each of the sheep; all facets of the spiritual creation, *omnes gentes*, are to come together.

These two concerns occupy and are at the heart of Catholic ecumenism. The phrase "social Catholicism" would be unacceptable to our Catholic brethren if it was not in any case tautological, but the same is true of "ecumenical Catholicism". Ecumenism and Catholicism are the same thing. Adjectives like social and ecumenical are simply aids to impel the intelligence into a deeper understanding of the essence of Catholicity.

Catholic ecumenism is grounded on what might be called

the "potential" concept of Catholicity. When we say that the Church is catholic we are not of course saying that she contains at this time all peoples, nor even that if all peoples should be immediately and miraculously converted they would at once find themselves at home in the Church as she is today. What we are saying is that the substantial form of the Church is such that if this highly improbable conversion took place nothing *essential* would have to be changed in its teachings, worship or government. The Church has the potential capacity of including within her unity all human diversity: that is why she calls herself catholic, and why those who work towards the gradual realization of that potentiality are called ecumencial. Suppose all men on earth wished to enter therein; what would happen? The living cathedral,

quae celsa de viventibus
saxis ad astra tollitur,

would enlarge her fabric, building on to the porch, extending the chapels, heightening the towers. She would be renewed and in that movement would rid herself of the tuneless choir, the buyers and sellers in the forecourt, the meaningless ornament, the relics of another age; but she would keep the same form, and that form would be more beautiful in being more complete. Ecumenism aims at healing the breach between potentiality and actuality, or, more precisely, between developments due to historical factors and the wholeness that can be.

This is the meaning of Catholic ecumenism. Non-Catholic ecumenism uses the same term but not in the same sense. There are two paths here, converging no doubt, but different. On the day when they come together there will be no more ecumenism because there will no longer be this problem of the Church's nature; those times which were the occasion of the divergences will have reached their end. It is for our separated brethren in the World Council to elaborate a definition of what ecumenism means to them. Non-Catholic ecumenism is practical in character rather than theoretical;

Pope Paul VI with Patriarch Athenagoras I in the Apostolic Delegation of Jerusalem at the time of the Pope's visit to the Holy Land.

The editor, Luis Romeu, secretary of the John XXIII Ecumenical Centre at the Pontifical University of Salamanca, with the Russian Orthodox observers at the Second Session of Vatican II. Archpriest Borovoy is in the centre.

Catholic ecumenism is based on principles before practice. But from now on, we, who with them are praying in our hearts, have to look outwards, and it is with real sympathy that we observe the urge towards communion, shared worship especially in the Lord's Supper, which moves that great organization. Non-Roman ecumenical gatherings are not expressions of the end of Reformation (which in a sense is a permanent thing, even in the Roman Church herself) but they do show the end of a spirit of separation, secession, making protestation. Considerable divergences often exist still, but there is now an over-riding wish for unity.

[This contribution was translated by Rachel Attwater.]

The Prior of Taizé, Roger Schutz, with Metropolitan Meliton at the inauguration of the Church of Reconciliation, Taizé.

Thomas Holland, Bishop of Salford

The Right Rev. Thomas Holland, ordained 1933, coadjutor bishop of Portsmouth 1960, bishop of Salford since September 1964.

I was sent to Rome in 1933 to complete my theological studies at the Gregorian. The Beda College (originally founded by Pius IX for convert clergymen training for the priesthood) became my home for three years.

Among the clergymen then studying at the Beda was an American, Henry Pearce, who possessed a remarkable collection of books and documents relating to the Anglo-Catholic movement in the period 1890–1925. (Bishop d'Herbigny assured Pearce that the collection was unique and should never be dispersed.)

I read the literature of the movement and met men who had worked in it. From the beginning Anglo-Catholic leaders (for example, Pusey) had claimed that the Holy Spirit was working in and through the Anglican Establishment to restore Catholic faith and devotion.

The idea grew in my mind that a useful subject for a doctorate thesis would be to examine the theological possibilities of such a claim. The title might be: "*De Actione Spiritus Sancti in Ecclesiis separatis* with special reference to the Anglo-Catholic Movement."

The idea was not greatly welcomed. Professors said the subject was too vast and undocumented. Eventually Fr S. Tromp, S.J., agreed to supervise my efforts. Entirely through his helpful guidance, the thesis was at length written, and accepted by the Gregorian. Fr Tromp's own work on the Mystical Body provided the framework for developing my ideas.

The thesis was of no general value, but at least it gave the writer a life-long interest in what might be called "the assimilative action" of the Holy Spirit outside the Church. One came to know the fervour with which, for example, the Octave of Prayer for Unity was observed in Anglican communities. From 1948 onwards, as a member of the Catholic Missionary Society (founded to explain the Catholic Faith in England and Wales to our separated brethren), one found oneself often speaking on the same platform with Anglicans and Nonconformists. The hierarchy entrusted the C.M.S. with the work of implementing the Instruction of the Holy Office (*Ecclesia Catholica*, 20 December, 1949). One came to know the work of Mgr Willebrands and others.

I dare say none of this work would have ever come my way, nor would I have tried to do my thesis in 1933 in the face of a certain amount of discouragement, but for a much earlier interest as a youth in the conversion of England. I must thank the zealous priests who instilled this interest by their own prayerful example. We grew up with a deep longing for our country to be united again in the profession of the true Faith. Forty years ago the general atmosphere was so cold and hostile, it was only possible to think of individual conversions. Through the warmth of the Holy Spirit, other approaches are now possible. I know, of course, that an ecumenist, as such, is not directly concerned with conversion. But in his heart he must long and pray for the time and the moment *quae Pater posuit in sua potestate*.

But what does one expect now, at the present time, of the Ecumenical Movement? Frankly, nothing sensational. In fact one's own instinct would be to wonder if anything sensational in this field is likely to be supremely constructive. One *can* point to events which are at once sensational and productive of great good, for example, Lord Fisher's visit to the Pope or the presence of non-Catholic observers at the Council.

This latter event both Cardinal Bea and Oscar Cullmann

explicitly called a "miracle". But if you study the remarkable press-interview of 23 November 1963 in which Cullmann used this generous phrase, you will find matter for serious reflection. With a simplicity and honesty that do him great credit, this gifted exegete goes on to describe his reactions as he listens to the debates in the Council aula. Even if the renewal of the Church is achieved by the Council, one has to remember, says Cullmann, "ce renouveau sera réalisé dans le *cadre* et sur la *base* du *catholicisme* . . . il subsistera une différence importante entre nous et le catholicisme, donc aussi le catholicisme renouvelé par ce Concile." The dialogue must go on, he concludes, but in much more favourable conditions.

I do not think one can say much more than that. The lamented Pope John said that our best contribution to the Ecumenical Movement would be our own renewal in the spirit of the Gospel. "They will understand us better then, and we shall understand them."

Confidence now exists on both sides; the way is opening to greater mutual understanding, but the basic differences remain. It would be a mistake to judge the whole field by the complete understanding that exists in one or two sectors. The community of Taizé, certain groups of Anglicans, others in Holland and elsewhere, understand us almost to the point of compenetration. But are they sufficiently characteristic of the world of our separated brethren?

We in England at least are glad that now we can conduct the dialogue not with those only who are closest in sympathy, but with all sections of the Anglicans and Nonconformists. The difficulties are at once greater, but the work is more realistic, more commensurate with the problem as a whole.

We can all learn from the example of the German theologians who have spent years of dialogue with the Lutherans simply in establishing a common meaning of the terms to be employed in theological discussion. Those years were well spent.

Perhaps after the Council the *tempo* may be accelerated. But there will be need for patient, thorough work and prayer.

Antonio María Javierre

Antonio María Javierre was born in Huesca. He entered the Salesians at an early age. He is now professor and Dean of the Theological faculty of the Salesian Pontifical College in Turin.

THE THREE DIMENSIONS OF ECUMENISM

Those responsible for this book already know only too well my strong resistance to writing these pages. And I had many motives for offering such resistance. I would like to think that the majority of my compatriots would feel a similar repugnance. Nevertheless, I consider it highly desirable to swell the ecumenical ranks with some Spanish names. They may not be able to contribute anything new in the way of experience, but their mere presence brings to the dialogue a Catholic dimension that dispenses with any sort of barrier. Ecumenism ceases to be an imported product. It is Spanish by the mere fact of being Catholic; *res nostra agitur*. It matters little how many kilometres separate the Puerta del Sol from the centres of the Protestant or Orthodox worlds. The tragedy of separation weighs equally heavily on the people of Madrid and Athens. Does one feel less pain the greater the distance of a wound from the brain? As a spiritual body it is extremely difficult to define the shades of difference between the word "Catholicism" and genuine "ecumenism". Thus it is impossible to imagine a single corner of the world where there is not sympathy for the desire for union which is making itself felt throughout Christendom at the present time.

Nevertheless, this dynamism strikes at the most vital region of our existence. According to Leenhardt, the famous exegete of Geneva University, ecumenism is reduced in the final instance to a problem of faith. In the course of an interview that I shall never forget, we had occasion to analyse the deep motives imposed by different interpretations of a certain verse in the New Testament. Leenhardt, with implacable severity, excluded a multitude of hypotheses, which were nevertheless quite probable. Firstly, exegetic differences cannot be explained on psychological grounds, since the barriers of polemics of the past have now given place to an excellent comprehensiveness everywhere. Secondly, the phenomenon cannot be attributed to aberrations in the interpretation of history, because careful sifting of the facts relating to separation results in conclusions that are at any rate convergent. Thirdly, dissension cannot be resolved by resorting to the metaphysical formulas proposed at the Amsterdam assembly in 1948. Even if we were to accept that rather oversimplified approach of "Catholic" horizontals contrasted with "Protestant" verticals, we would still have to explain the reason for those preferences, which, it should be added, are not exclusive. Leenhardt concluded by reducing the motives of our differences to the area of faith. It is faith that colours the horizon in ways that are diametrically opposed. The fact of having been born in the midst of a Catholic or Calvinist family determines for ever one's peculiar view of Christ and the Church. The treasure placed in his hands by Providence is not the individual's responsibility, but it is his solemn duty to preserve it intact till the end of his days without any compromising fluctuations from one faith to another.

I am afraid that Leenhardt's attitude embodies a double objection which is by no means insignificant. Is it not bordering on paradoxical that there are millions of Christians everlastingly subjected to error "by their loyalty to Christ"? Is it permissible to neutralize ecumenical efforts in the name of loyalty to a Christ who imposed programmatic unity on his flock?

Conflicts such as these serve as excellent examples of the depth of the ecumenical problem. No sooner does one penetrate the surface sentimentality than one finds oneself immersed in the world of faith. My conviction that ecumenism's most urgent task is one of methodological order dates from this time. It is imperative that the flood of energy recently released in the Christian world in a very unsystematic and unco-ordinated manner should be quickly given direction.

This explains why my personal diary contains so many methodological observations. They are grouped naturally around the three aspects of the act of faith. An ecumenical undertaking which claims to be completely efficient cannot ignore, firstly, that the harmonious act of faith, as imagined by the separated Christians, is a gift of *grace* that man can obtain, at most, by means of humble prayer. Secondly, that the act of faith, if it is to be a perfectly *free* decision, needs a lubricant that will eliminate the dangerous frictions that emerge from the dark world of sentiment. Thirdly, so that the act of faith should be *reasonable* as befits an authentic human gesture, it is necessary to bring to light that difficult visibility of which Pascal spoke; clear enough to allow man to direct his steps without groping and discreet enough not to trespass upon the hidden realm of mystery.

I originally intended to extract selected episodes from my diary. At the last moment I decided to sum up its permanent lesson from the methodological point of view in three condensed notes. It is necessary to pray, smooth out misunderstandings and put theology unconditionally at the service of ecumenism. I do not know if my answers are satisfactory, but I am not prepared to hide facts that many people leave unsaid, perhaps because they consider them too obvious.

I. Ecclesiastical liturgy, the fundamental requirement of healthy ecumenism

The recent conciliar Constitution on Sacred Liturgy names ecumenism amongst the final stages of the plan for unity. Really it is only selecting one aspect deeply involved in its essence. Because ecumenism and liturgy have always been very closely related.

My diary does not give the exact date on which the first instructions for ecumenical prayer came into my hands.

It was on the occasion of the octave of prayer for unity that I first came across the name of Father Wattson. I realize now that it was a subtle stroke of Providence to allow me that "encounter" with Orthodox, Anglicans and Protestants, not on the battle front but in the quiet, intimate seclusion of a Catholic chapel resounding at that time with the echo of Christ's *ut unum sint*.

The concessions made by the Holy See in the instruction *De motione oecumenica* provoked stirring criticism, which aroused anxiety in those of us who were then studying theology. I could not guess then the sharp tingle of emotion and even anguish I was to experience later in reciting the Lord's Prayer together with separated brethren. I had the feeling that they were new words, that stuck in my throat, and which, though forcefully uttered, remained floating in the atmosphere without the spirit managing to collate proximity and distance, and without the heart resigning itself to breaking the spell of a spiritual interference as deep as it was ephemeral.

At ecumenical assemblies I always found a privileged place in the programme set aside for prayer. They produced moments of intense fervour. For me the most suggestive are the most spontaneous; a pause imposed during a discussion by the group president in order to obtain a divine solution from above when no human one offered itself, is an unforgettable moment, and one which places ecumenism in its authentic centre of gravitation. Max Thurian caused me to share his dissatisfaction at the New Delhi assembly. He was longing for an authentic cathedral much more warm and solid than anything suggested by the ephemeral Shamiana. Montreal, on the other hand, offered us a unique evening in the history of the ecumenical movement. For the first time there was amongst the leaders of the various faiths a cardinal of the Catholic Church, who was glad of the opportunity to preach to the whole of Christendom and lead the common prayers for unity. But we should not think that ecumenical prayer has reached its greatest heights.

Montreal could not avoid the tragedy of division before the eucharistic table. Separation becomes particularly unbearable at this moment. Some wanted to break down barriers and make lightning advances. I continue to think that we must give infinite thanks to our Lord for the authentic sign that he has left us in the Eucharist. We must not forge illusions for ourselves.

We must intensify our prayers. On our knees it is easier to evoke the distance of the absent brethren without acerbity; on our knees we can measure more accurately the deep gulf that separates us; on our knees we appreciate our own impotence more and in Christ's hands we can abandon ourselves more readily to the task of ecumenism. It is no small victory to restore to his lips the prayer of the Last Supper: *ut unum sint.*

II: *Meetings of the different faiths, a magnificent pedagogy of comprehension*

It is not easy to reconstruct the complexity of a life from a repertory of propositions of dogma nor to interpret accurately the symbolic books of a faith except within the framework of life. It was Professor D'Espine, at that time president of the Swiss Federation of Protestant Churches, who suggested to me an unexpected exegetical guide—take an active part in the ecumenical meetings. We held friendly discussions at his Geneva home on the records of the Evanston assembly. I pointed out to him my profound amazement at the reformed Church's acceptation of the Lutheran formula *iustus simul et peccator* applied to the Church. Professor D'Espine tried in vain to persuade me that the ideological inflexions of which I was accusing Evanston did not exist. I say in vain because, to my mind, his arguments sounded purely evasive. He bore with me very patiently, finally concluding the matter with a sentence which I committed in full to my diary: "You Catholics have an innate tendency to interpret ecumenical texts like council documents. They are, however, very different. You would have to be present at their birth at one of our assemblies to inject into your exegesis the same elasticity that we put into their composition." It goes without saying that, at the time, I was not satisfied with his answer, but it did sow the seeds of a deep curiosity in my mind, and I have since had the good fortune to satisfy it. I can assure you that his advice, far from being arbitrary, was the product of a long experience. Outside the context of life it is very difficult to avoid excesses of exegesis.

On the other hand, it is not enough to outline an exegesis in order to reconstruct a life. This is especially true when there are facts involved which, in one way or another, obstruct one's vision. I have not had an opportunity to compare my fellow scholar's reactions to the study of the Reformation. Ecclesiastical history classes repeatedly aroused in my mind the same question that I was to encounter later in the history of philosophy. Is it possible, I wondered, for men universally acknowledged as brilliant thinkers to be the authors of the paltry collections of assertions to be found in our philosophical "anthologies"? A personal reading of their works convinced me that that was, in fact, what they had said, but not only that, and in a context which gave a particular relief to their doctrine. In the light of reputable history books, which do not disguise their apologetic intention, I wondered whether it was permissible to reduce the revolution started by Luther to the simple revolt of an independent, lascivious, angry and heretical friar. I suspected, not without good reason, that there was a multitude of hidden variations, and I tried to state them precisely. Secondly, I do not want to suggest that I put a grain of "sympathy" into my study of Protestantism. It had been nipped in the bud by a sad episode that I tried in vain to forget. Even today I still have a clear memory of the unpleasant impression made upon me by a meeting with a former student at a Catholic religious college, who later became a Protestant. He came one day to ask me for a book by Don Bosco, for whom he showed a sincere admiration. I was happy to obtain it for him, and did so with a flood of ingenuous hopes that, at this distance, I find it hard to define. He received the gift with much pleasure. He was dispensing the accepted expressions of gratitude, when he discovered among its pages a small print of the saint. He suddenly lost control, and, his courteous manner giving way to the most unbridled vulgarity, he accused Catholicism of idolatry, superstition, and ignorance, finally stamping on the print in front of me. Today I am grateful to our Lord for the bitterness of that moment. Do I have to confess that my first encounters with the Protestants were, as a result of my studies, more full of prejudice than ingenuous romanticism?

I do not remember having ever evoked such an episode at Geneva, Lausanne, Turin, Niederaltaich, New Delhi or Montreal. It would seem quite out of place there. Meetings between the different faiths have the virtue of laying bare the soul, and those that find harmony there show an edifying love of Christ, and moving good will. Wounds such as mine heal up as if by magic, and spontaneously an intimate, sincere and profound understanding arises.

It is not that ecumenical assemblies temporarily suspend one's own convictions. On the contrary, it has been noticed repeatedly that the opposite is the case: the Calvinist becomes more Calvinistic, the Lutheran feels his Lutheranism more sincerely, the Orthodox professes his Orthodoxy more intensely. All this is done without causing any offence to one's neighbour, whose purity of intention is known to all. What, then, is the secret of such meetings? To put it simply, they are a magnificent exercise in the art of understanding. They set out to redeem an element which is indispensable to the solution of the problem. The controversies, polarized perhaps a little emphatically towards the truth, do not consider sufficiently the point of view of the interlocutor. There are those who say ironically that they are pursuing a goal of love by means of an implacable dialectic of interdenominational hatred. I do not like to oversimplify extremely complex historical situations. The important thing to realize is that ecumenism needs both poles, and that the ecumenical meetings have recovered one of them that has long been passed over.

Much has already been done. I know very well from experience that, today, the Catholic priest's *celebret* is a magnificent passport in Protestant countries. However, much still remains to be done. Our Lord does not allow me the sin of ingenuousness in this matter. On my return from New Delhi, with the vision of an unexpectedly wonderful meeting still before me, I had to return to the sad reality of divisions that we had only suppressed in our hopes in India. In Jerusalem, indeed at the Holy Sepulchre itself, I was to have personal experience of the sadness of the separation of the Christian faiths, which govern the most revered church in Christendom. I had to leave the church by a small window because in order to avoid countless dissensions the Christians had decided to leave the keys in the hands of an Arab, whose job it was to open and lock up from outside. On that particular day his watch must have been a few minutes fast.

The ecumenical movement has succeeded in establishing contacts on a world-wide scale. Without the lubricative agency of contacts, understanding, and of mutual trust it is utopian to hope for a solution. The history of relations between Catholics and Orthodox shows, on the other hand, that agreement at the summit is not enough. Without more general backing from the community there is no solid basis for definite solutions, and therefore these exercises in the art of understanding that I have spoken of become all the more valuable.

III. *The Second Vatican Council. The general academy of ecumenism*

As a result of the International Eucharistic Congress at Munich a week of living together was held for the different faiths at Niederaltaich under the auspices of the "Una Sancta" movement. The theme of the real presence of Christ at the Eucharist produced an exceptionally lively assembly. Dr Ritter could not resist either the blackboard full of theological formulas, or the atmosphere, rarefied more by the clashes of ideas than by tobacco smoke. He stood up with an energetic flourish and, turning his back on the formulas under discussion, gave the audience a spirited harangue. If I remember correctly, he suggested the liturgy as the most hopeful course for ecumenical dialogue. Carried away by the fervour of his oratory, he forgot the condition of his improvised cathedra, and through repeatedly leaning against the blackboard he eventually transferred all the theological formulas to the back of his jacket. A young pastor, with a brush in his hand, took it upon himself to demonstrate to the assembly the ancient duty of deacons. While he was engaged in this, various pithy comments were heard: "Dr Ritter's contagious eloquence", remarked one colleague, "has a very simple secret: all that is needed is to turn our backs olympically on theological exercises and everything will be simplified." "Quite the reverse", retorted a second one immediately, "the efficacy of this speaker lies in the fact that his formulas, so simple in appearance, are backed by the strongest theological reasonings."

Ecumenism without theology? Ecumenism with theology? The answer is quite simple; reason intervenes in the act of faith. It occupies one of the three points of the triangle. I agree that it is the least of them, but it remains indispensable. Therefore the solution of the ecumenical problem cannot be the monopoly of theologians; but it is also utopian to hope to find it outside theology. Firstly, this was confirmed for me by a parish priest, who was as zealous in the pursuit of his apostolic duties as he was unhampered by books and theories. Following an unusually animated discussion at a periodical meeting between Catholics and Waldensians, he said to me, "Father, perhaps you would be interested in hearing my own case, which I myself find very strange. I am perfectly aware that our meetings are not designed to convert anyone, nevertheless, in spite of myself I have to admi that I have been wholly converted . . . to theology." Secondly I returned to my thoughts on reason in the act of faith throughout the second session of the Vatican Council. Several of the interventions on the subject of ecumenism might have left the impression in less well informed minds that knowledge and mutual understanding are all that is needed to resolve the ecumenical problem completely. "No," said one of the English-speaking members of the council forcefully, "not at all. In my diocese the frontier of faith between Catholics and Anglicans strikes through the heart of families. Although there is perfect love and understanding between fathers and sons, loving husbands and wives, and united brothers and sisters, some may be Catholics and others Anglicans. Mere understanding and love cannot entirely resolve the problem, which remains tragically intact." I greatly enjoyed that realistic contribution. The ecumenical gatherings have brilliantly revived the rights of the interlocutor. Will it be for the Vatican only to throw into relief those that correspond to the truth?

Catholicism has never relegated truth to second place, but clearly it now sees it in a new perspective. There is talk of a change in its attitude to ecumenism, and there is nothing strange in that. If it is certain that the pastoral application implies a projecting of immutable principles on to historical situations, it is clear that a constant rectifying of its methods is not only legitimate but necessary in the face of the continual fluidity of history.

All this would seem to suggest that the Catholic Church is determined to initiate an authentic dialogue. Why should it not be accepted if the interlocutor, whatever his attitude in the past, today professes absolute respect for the truth of Christ and offers his sincere collaboration in the task of bringing Christians together? The precept of loyalty to the deposit of faith—*tenete traditiones*—does not compel the Church to forget the mandate included in the *negotiamini dum venio*. Was it going to ruin the atmosphere of mutual understanding that the spirit of Christ has created in the hearts of all who claim to be his followers?

The Vatican Council has set out faithful to St Paul's dictum: *veritatem facientes in caritate.* Firstly, *truth* is an inalienable principle for Catholicism. Can it forget its founder is divine Truth incarnate? I find in my diary moving notes concerning the attitude of absolute loyalty of the members of the Council. Secondly, *charity* is the contemporary style of dialogue, which contains prospects of change from the attitude of controversy in the past. Thirdly, St Paul's *facientes* points to the promising dynamism with which the Church appears rejuvenated to the astonished eyes of the world.

After the last Faith and Order conference, which met last summer in Montreal, Professor Von Allmen, no doubt disillusioned by the lack of results obtained in the ecclesiastical ministry section, whose activities he followed so generously and competently, confided in me pessimistically, casting the responsibility for the future of ecumenism on to the Vatican Council: "Our movement has reached an insuperable limit. We have come to a dead end. If the Catholic Church does not extend its hand to us, it is pointless to pursue our efforts. They are condemned to sterility."

I thought instinctively of Von Allmen when I witnessed the enthusiastic reception that the majority of the Fathers accorded to the ecumenical scheme. The hopes engendered everywhere by the Council are great, and are based on very robust foundations. The Vatican will continue to be the leading school of ecumenism as long as it effectively preserves the methodological preoccupation centred on the three points of the act of faith. Firstly, there are intense daily prayers for the unity of Christians. Secondly, there is established in the Vatican a current of reciprocal understanding with the separated brethren, who are symbolically present in the Council chamber and take an active part when it comes to drawing up the texts. Thirdly, at the second Vatican Council the best theologians of the Catholic world are working to discover formulas that will satisfy the truth, which is one, without detriment to the rights of charity. The infallible assistance of the Holy Spirit is assured. In my opinion ecumenism is still only beginning, but this tactical deployment on the part of the Council fills me with optimism. Respect for the problem's triple dimension is a guarantee of having recognized the magnitude of its methodological difficulties.

One of the Council members alluded to the three stages of the ecumenical journey. It has its *purgative* stage, for there are many hills and valleys to be levelled. Next comes the *illuminative* stage, which is largely the responsibility of the theologians, whose task is to let in light where formerly there was only darkness. Only later, when the two preceding stages have been completed, comes the *unitive* stage, a moment reserved for our Lord.

Spain must not remain outside this activity for two convergent reasons; ecumenism needs Spain, and Spain cannot dispense with ecumenism.

1. The Taizé bulletin *Aujourd'hui* recently published an article entitled "Spain, the ill-loved". The author stated the thesis that

> it is necessary to *love* men in order to understand them from within; this deals with a fundamental attitude. Now Spain is not well loved. Both the Catholics and the Protestants have disclosed to visiting brethren the agitation of a wounded soul, because the Spaniard has had to resign himself for many years to living in isolation, criticized, judged, rejected by Europe and by the world, even by Christians themselves, including foreign Catholics. Like a misunderstood child and impelled by her typically Castilian *honor*, Spain, without saying a word, has withdrawn within herself. Why should not sweetness and love be redoubled now in order to establish dialogue with Spaniards? And it is so very easy to engage in the language of love with such a great-hearted people! There would be so much to say about Spain's Christian virtues, the fervour of her prayer, the spirit of abstraction from worldly affairs, of meditation and the practice of hospita-

lity. But what should be underlined and repeated time and again is that the Spanish temperament, capable of deep passions, is fundamentally *generous*. In such fertile ground the seeds of the Bible and ecumenism can be expected to germinate and bear excellent fruit. Spanish Christians, so richly endowed, are called upon to inject new blood into the ecumenical movement, and, who knows, perhaps to play an unexpected and decisive part in the march towards unity.

Generous words which reveal that rare understanding that comes from "sympathy" and love. Certainly ecumenism today is not overendowed with theological impetus, concerned as it is with balances of a sociological nature. A contribution from the Spanish theologians with their speculative temperament would surely be providential.

2. I do not intend to omit the counterpart. The Spaniards must be convinced, whether they like it or not, that their behaviour has a world-wide projection and reflects decisively on the progress of ecumenism. I quote as my only documentary evidence a page that I read months ago, and which remains imprinted on my soul. It concerns a review of John XXIII's encyclical *Pacem in terris*. In contrast to a gigantic chorus of praise, the author made very serious reservations: "I am unable to pinpoint exactly the error in the pontifical argument; but there is no doubt that the document contains a sophism. In fact, if the Pope's thesis were exact, the function of a truly Catholic life would be sociological perfection. From which it follows that greater perfection in social institutions corresponds with greater liberty of action for Catholicism. Well now, if there is one country where Catholicism acts without hindrance from any class, and where the doctrine of the Church can be carried to its ultimate conclusion, it is in Spain. And I ask, is there a single individual in the Anglo-Saxon world who looks with envy upon Spain's social achievements, or who considers the present situation in Spain a sociological ideal?" There is no

point in commenting on the text, which I have not, furthermore, translated entirely. But it leaves a smart in the soul and makes one aware of our privileged significance in the ecumenical world. We should know that Germans and Dutch study the theses of their own Catholic interlocutors, but they take a sideways glance at Spain to learn about Catholicism in action. We must be conscious of this, and not allow our brethren to suffer moments of anguish in the front line on our account.

The three slopes of ecumenism have very different variations of colour. Spanish Catholicism has a specific task in connection with the three points of the act of faith and it would not be easy to find a substitute. Does not each cell have a specific function in the life of an organism? The ecumenical impulse has no significance unless it is expressed in terms of a mystical body.

[This contribution was translated by A. F. Price.]

Carlos Malik

Dr Carlos Malik comes from the Lebanon and belongs to the Orthodox Church. He is Foreign Minister of his country and was named President of U.N.O. in 1959. He is a Professor at the American University at Beirut.

UNITY AND HISTORY

I

The problem of Christian unity is inseparable from the problem of the Church. Christian unity is in effect Church unity. For some Christians can claim that in a certain vague sense they are already "united" with all other Christians in that they all have a special relationship to Jesus Christ. It is therefore the nature and authority of the Church that is here in question. Unity is fundamentally determined by ecclesiology.

This raises in turn the problem of God's relations to history and indeed the problem of the nature of history itself. How does God act in history? How has he acted? Do we just get up every morning, read the Bible, say our prayers, and then God, there and then, directly deals with us, independently of anything in the past, independently even of his past dealings with other men? Or is there a meaning and a reality to the authentic transmission of the tradition from generation to generation and culture to culture? How has the past mediated God to us? What is the content of human historical solidarity? What is the content of the divine historical economy? Concretely, what do we owe to the past? And this very Bible, where did it come from? Who has certified its revealed character? Our theories of unity and history therefore mutually determine each other.

Ecclesiology and what I might term "historiology" are at the base of any serious quest for Christian unity. Seek first the nature of the Church and the nature of history, and the problem of Christian unity becomes perfectly clear to you. What did Christ intend the Church *to be* and how has this intended being *actually existed in history*?—these are the two ultimate questions. The truth of these two questions does not arise from any arbitrary decision: the truth positively and independently exists, and, if humbly sought, can be ascertained.

II

In a very real sense unity reigned until 1054. Two questions then must be answered: what was it that constituted that unity while it lasted, and what happened when the Great Schism between East and West occurred? No man can answer these two questions *a priori*; he must make use of the excellent existing historical and doctrinal studies.

Since Christ certainly wants unity, it is not reasonable to suppose that the unity that once reigned for a thousand years was not in accordance with the will of Christ. Therefore the pattern of that unity must serve as our norm. We are not starting from zero wondering what the will of Christ is: we have a thousand years behind us—and therefore "before" us—of actual, concrete manifestation of that will.

This raises the question of doctrinal evolution since then. This is a very difficult question, but those who sincerely put unity above every other consideration, except the consideration of the truth, and conformity to the will of Christ, will not fail, with the help of the Holy Ghost, to find ways and means for solving even this most crucial question. I have proposals on this point, but who am I to make them? By its very nature this problem can be handled only between duly constituted authorities of corporate Churches.

The craving for unity and the pressure of the Holy Ghost to that end are among the clearest phenomena of this age. In importance I place this matter above every other contemporary excitement. It follows that no problem connected with the question of unity is too delicate to be faced and discussed: everything must be lifted into the open, everything must be humbly gone into—tradition, the Bible, the Councils, the Pope, the question of the episcopacy, the hierarchy, the liturgy, Protestant principles, the teaching authority of the Church, cultural and political matters—absolutely everything.

People rightly worry about all sorts of terrible problems today, but let the Christians constitute one real Body of Christ, and no problem then will be beyond their power to solve or to control.

Absolute understanding, absolute humility, absolute charity, utter patience and the total overcoming of the pride and self-will of man by the grace and love of Jesus Christ—without these no unity can be achieved or maintained. But these things are well within the power of the Holy Ghost.

Those who, having been baptized in the name of the Father and the Son and the Holy Ghost, love Jesus Christ above everything else, and, while unworthy, nevertheless seek to obey him, live under the necessity of wholeheartedly praying and working for unity according to his will. The believer can aspire to no greater reward than to be granted to see a measure of true unity realized in his lifetime.

Patriarch Maximos IV

His Beatitude, Cardinal Maximos IV Saygh, the Melchite Patriarch, is Patriarch of Antioch and all the East, Alexandria and Jerusalem. As head of the Melchites, Maximos IV is the only patriarch of the Byzantine rite. He has been called "the most outspoken of the Eastern bishops". Born in 1878, he was ordained in 1905 and was appointed to the Metropolitan see of Tyre in 1919. He has visited the U.S.A. on many occasions, the first Melchite parish there having been founded in 1895. He was elected to the patriarchate in 1947. At Vatican II he has played an active role and has especially urged the need for a non-Roman approach to essential questions. In his writings he has always stressed the universality of the Church. He was created Cardinal in 1965.

UNION AND ECUMENISM

After centuries of unconcern or confessional strife it is good to observe today that the problem of the reunion of the Churches has at last taken sufficient shape to force itself on the Christian conscience.

It is true that there are still many Christians who regard reunion as a beautiful dream or an ideal as unattainable as world peace. I am not of this number. Yet those who hold that Christ's prayer for the unity of all Christians could not be vain, and who "dare to believe" in it, are impeded by a disconcerting dissimilitude in conceptions of that unity. The fact of the matter is that, in their common and fervent desire for unity, all Christians are not in agreement on the nature of the goal they are seeking.

It is not my purpose here to examine the very varied standpoints of Anglicans, Protestants and indeed of our own Orthodox brethren. But as Catholics hold it, Christ established his Church on the apostles and their successors the bishops, acting individually or collectively under the primacy of Peter and his successor the Bishop of Rome. That spiritual authority is attested by Christ's promise to Peter. The Church is, then, an organic body, with members and government at once individual and collegial, whose cohesion is ultimately assured by communion with a visible head, the Roman pontiff. It follows that separation from this visible head, in whom is embodied the Church's infallibility, can never be sanctioned. In consequence, union of Churches is necessarily conceived fundamentally in terms of communion with the Roman pontiff and through him with all the bishops, successors of the apostles, who are united to him.

The Catholic Church, in her members, pastors and even her chief pastor, must bear her own large share of responsibility in the various internal crises which led to Christian secessions. She has in her members, pastors and even her chief pastor been defective in directing herself towards positive holiness, and in her striving towards the universal, has been constantly crossed by human, national, political and cultural passions and interests.

The wrongs done by Catholics in the past must also be recognized by themselves. There is nothing shameful in this; it is the great heart which acknowledges its own faults. So, then, Rome must express due recognition of these things.

The very real Catholic responsibilities in the history of the secessions which have divided Christians help us to understand how schism came about; they do not justify its continued existence.

There are necessary and indeed urgent reforms to be carried out, and we must trust the Lord to bring about their accomplishment, so that no follower of his may want the grace of union through our fault or that of our brethren.

To quicken steps towards union, ecumenism proposes a method which is not so much a slow and gradual erosion of sister-Churches as a spirit of apostleship which is more in harmony with the Gospel ideal of brotherhood. Above and beyond the legitimate endeavours for the reconciliation of individuals, there is greater and greater scope for a combined exertion towards understanding between dissident Christians, the drawing together of Churches as such through mutual respect and charity.

The ecumenical spirit is rooted in considerations of a purely religious nature. The unity which we are seeking has nothing to do with a simple coalition of the Churches in pursuance of certain common interests. If union should make us more powerful it is in order that we may more powerfully love all men in Christ who wishes us to be "one". The ecumenical spirit consists first in the quest for truth for its own sake. This requires a profound attachment to our own Church, thus excluding the false irenicism of those who claim to be unconcerned with doctrinal differences, the interconfessionalism of those who believe it possible to subscribe to all Churches on the grounds that it is not necessary to submit to any one in particular to know Christ, or the rigid uniformity of those who are "more Catholic than the pope". At the same time we must recognize our own responsibility, individual and collective, in the quarrels which divided our forefathers, the spiritual qualities and gifts proper to other confessions, and the human and supernatural enrichment of which their separation has deprived the Christian community as a whole. Ecumenism is also a spirit of love which compels the renunciation of sectarianism, the cessation of all partisan polemics, the stripping ourselves of prejudice with the courteous willingness to help others to be rid of theirs, to seek to meet in all fields and all ways which do not impair the rights of truth itself.

The visible unity of all baptized Christians is the ultimate goal of all our labours. But it would seem that this unity must be pursued collectively rather than individually. The ruptures were not the work of private individuals but the cruel result of increasing division between minds and hearts, which revealed itself on certain occasions and through the agency of Church leaders who were in themselves neither better nor worse than others.

It is apparent, also, that Christian reunion is not going to fall from the skies one day, ready-made like a prefabricated house. We are embarking not so much on the search for a long-lost precious stone as the slow, patient and laborious rebuilding of a great structure which our forefathers shook so often and so violently that in the end it gave way. Need it be added, then, that our task is that of preparing the ground for rebuilding?

Ecumenism is to union what the road is to its goal. Ecumenism is not a doctrine; nor is it an end in itself in which we should rest. Union cannot be achieved on the basis of the lowest common denominator. It is to be found at the conclusion of a long journey on which all Christians together will have truly sought to learn through charity, faithfulness and humility what is indeed the will of the Lord for his Church.

[This contribution was translated by Rachel Attwater.]

Roger Mehl

Roger Mehl is chairman of the commission for ecumenical studies of the Federation of French Protestant Churches and a Professor at the University of Strasbourg. He is a member of the Faith and Order Commission of the World Council of Churches.

For many long ages a man could be a Christian without looking farther than the spire of his village church. That is no longer possible. The Church of God, of course, is in her fullness at Corinth: no one could contradict St Paul on that point. But if she is at Corinth, it is because the word of God is preached there in all its power and fullness, and the sacraments are administered. But all places where that happens are the Church, and the Church cannot be divided, because she is the Body of Christ. The Gospel cannot be preached in division, for if it is, whether we wish it or no, something is subtracted from the Gospel. It is no longer the power that reconciles, which out of two peoples has made one. Unity is an integral part of the Gospel message.

That seems to me the fundamental reason why a Christian cannot remain indifferent to the great historic movement which is passing through all the Christian Churches and impelling them, not only to re-establish a lost unity, not only to abolish out-dated barriers, but to show forth in all its fullness, in the world of today, the unity which is in Christ. That movement, which has taken shape in a number of institutions (the World Council of Churches, the present Vatican Council, the Roman Secretariat for Unity, the Pan-Orthodox Conference, etc.), is the ecumenical movement.

I like this qualification, "ecumenical", although originally the word had no ecclesiastical significance. It means "of the inhabited world". The Gospel is power of life and unity wherever the earth is inhabited, wherever men live.

The ecumenical demand is always present, of course, but today it has become in a way more perceptible, more palpable. For men are no longer partitioned off from one another. A planetary civilization is coming into being. Modern means of communication enable every human being to know what is happening all over the world. I cannot be indifferent to the fate of any man in the world. If a man is unjustly condemned thousands of miles away, we hear about it at once, and our intervention is sought on his behalf. The destiny of the Negroes of South Africa or of North America cannot leave us neutral. Our world has shrunk, and the time is past when profoundly different civilizations could develop side by side in mutual ignorance. The opportunity now offered us by history is to live in solidarity with all men. In spite of all the barriers, ideological, racial or national, which persist, and are sometimes growing even harder to pierce just because they feel themselves threatened, a really universal history is in process of taking shape. The secular world is in process of becoming catholic.

This sociological fact is in no way the foundation of ecumenism. In fact the ecumenical movement must be on its guard against becoming a pale reflection of a planetary civilization. But this fact is the *occasion* for the Church to become aware of her ecumenical task. Bossuet and Leibniz, even in their days, used to discuss the possibilities and conditions of the reunion of Christendom. But they were concerned only with that Western Christendom, that little sector, that little province of mankind. Today it is our duty to think of the unity of the Church on the scale of the whole planet.

But we must not imagine that the Christian Churches have only to agree among themselves and overcome the motives of separation, for a world-wide Church, strong, powerful and respected, at once to extend its jurisdiction over the whole world. If God wills that unity should be achieved (and of course things happen more slowly here than in the political world), the One Church is very likely to be only a small Church, that "little flock" of which our Lord spoke. In the human world of tomorrow, in a population of 4000 million, the Christian Churches, even if united, will be only a feeble minority. For in our modern civilization it will be less and less possible to be *born* a Christian. It will be necessary to become Christian by a personal decision to ask for baptism by oneself. I do not expect that unity is going to give the Church power. In a planetary civilization, shaped by technology and the values developed by a technological age, the Church of Christ will not be an established Church; less and less will she be an official institution, which men cannot do without, whose services men spontaneously feel they need. She will be a poor Church, perhaps even before she so chooses. She will be driven back to her origins, perhaps even without persecution, for the world only persecutes what threatens it. But she will be, as in her beginnings, a missionary Church.

The most interesting thing about ecumenism is that it demands and permits the rediscovery of the Church's missionary vocation. The separated Churches, of course, have never quite abandoned the missionary task, and we ought to be full of gratitude for what they have achieved, especially in the last two centuries. But the ecumenical movement has reminded them that, however we may define the Church, mission forms part of the essence of the Church, that a Church which has ceased to be missionary dies in its institutional ghetto, that by rediscovering its missionary vocation a Church encounters other Churches and is obliged to face the question of unity. In fact it has been on the mission field that the disunion of the Churches has been found intolerable: how can we proclaim the Gospel of our salvation in and by the one Christ, if the Churches remain divided, and their division permanently belies their preaching? In so far as in the West our ecclesiastical partitions have come to seem something normal, sanctioned by the diversity of our institutions, we have been progressively inoculated against the scandal of division, and so no longer feel it scandalous. But as soon as we have to turn towards "those outside", the scandal begins to sting again. The amalgamation of the World Council of Churches with the International Missionary Council (1961) is a sign of the refusal to tolerate this scandal indefinitely. One of the opportunities offered us by the present situation is that the younger Churches, founded by the missions, reproach us bitterly for having introduced our Western divisions into their lands. Our Churches stand before them as in the dock, and that is a good thing.

We find the same thing to be true, moreover, the more we are aware of the profound dechristianization of the West, and when our Churches understand that they can no longer confine themselves to cultivating the piety of their faithful members and preserving their flocks, but must undertake activity towards all who have lost all contact with the Gospel, who live, think and act according to other standards. For these people cannot be interested in the Gospel, if it is presented by Churches which are divided and competing, and must necessarily appear to be sects, even if their doctrine is not at all sectarian.

There can be no doubt that the path before us is a long one. We are still at the stage of the first stammerings of the ecumenical conscience. The obstacles which separate the Churches cannot be removed by a mere movement of good will. For they nearly always involve a question of truth, and that allows of no compromise or bargaining. But at least the Churches which have lived so long in isolation have ventured on a path of dialogue, whereas up to now they were content with controversy. True dialogue means that the Churches agree to listen to the questions put to them by the other Churches, agree to accept and give advice, to eliminate false problems from their dialogue, and to eliminate non-theological factors of division. The most undeniable success of the World Council of Churches has been that it has been able to organize such dialogue: the presence of non-Catholic observers at the Second Vatican Council proves that the Roman Church too desires dialogue. The recent Ecumenical Conference at Montreal (July 1962) has certainly not produced substantial results, but at least it has once again proved the possibility of a dialogue, and it is very rare that during such a dialogue some lines of convergence are not traced. The Vatican Council has not yet taken any decisive measures, but will no doubt do so in the Third Session. But up to now it is noticeable that it has been very careful to abstain from any decision which might delay ecumenical dialogue or make it more difficult.

What can we expect of the ecumenical movement? That question amounts to this: what can we expect of the ecumenical dialogue? To this a confident answer can be given. Everything can be expected from a dialogue, provided that it is not a dialogue of the deaf, each trying to speak louder than his partner and refusing to listen to what he says. But this risk should not be very great. As a fact the partners know from the beginning of the dialogue how much they have in common. Though separated, they are nonetheless brethren. Together they acknowledge the Lordship of Jesus Christ over the Church and over the world. Together they are moved by concern for the honour of God. Is that not a solid point of departure?

They know, moreover, that the Church does not live for herself but for the world, and that this world, for all its wealth and enthusiasm, is a world without hope, but also a world which longs to be shown the way of hope. For the sake of this world which God has so loved, the Churches must find the courage to engage in this difficult dialogue, to submit their traditions to question, to accept certain sacrifices. The final goal is, of course, the visible unity of the People of God. It is not for us to decide its time, but it would even now be an evidence of hope if, in sight of the world of today, the Churches were to give an example of an honest, lucid and truthful dialogue, of a sincere quest for unity, and still more of a perfect readiness to follow the promptings of the Holy Spirit. This readiness will involve certain sacrifices on all sides, make no doubt of it. But do the Churches not know that in any case their path leads through the Cross?

[This contribution was translated by P. J. Hepburne-Scott.]

Pierre Michalon, P.S.S.

Pierre Michalon is a Sulpician. He has taken on much of the work of the late Abbé Couturier at the centre for Christian Unity at Lyons.

I shall answer your question in a personal way.

In the town where I was brought up about 10,000 of the inhabitants were Protestants. When I was a child my family always showed profound respect for the sincerity of every man. More than that, my father liked to point out the Christian virtues of our non-Catholic brethren. All of us were trained to regard with the most unprejudiced eye those who often gave proof of great fervour. This was, of course, unusual forty years ago. On this point ours was not a timorous grandmotherly attitude which would consider the Protestants as strangers, who are to be respected, but have nothing fresh to give us.

It was in 1937. I had been a priest for four years. As a Sulpician I had dedicated my life to the training of the clergy. My superiors sent me to the Cevennes, the land of the "Protestant reserves", noted for vivid memories of the Wars of Religion. As Director of the Major Seminary at Viviers and Professor of Holy Scripture, I had priests of the region as my colleagues, and they will understand today how pained and surprised I was to find that they were completely cut off from the Protestant communities. They were quite unable to give me the slightest positive indication on the apostolic and spiritual vitality of this Protestantism of the Cevennes. The remarks I used to hear from them were terribly severe.

Whenever I happened to go on journeys in the mountains, I saw that the Protestants were as profoundly ignorant and prejudiced about Catholicism. Doors were shut in my face, help has been refused me. I have also seen Catholics turn aside from a case of sickness, because it was the mother of a Protestant family. And then I knew that, whatever the political and social causes may have been, the blood shed in the massacre of St Bartholomew was not yet forgotten.

This anguish filled my heart, for I could not shut my eyes to what it represented in the past and in the present. My theological and spiritual formation had been such that I had never thought of the Church as a closed citadel. I saw the influence of the Holy Spirit everywhere, I held firmly to the fundamental kinship created by baptism between all Christians. It was not in vain that I studied St Paul and St John. Perhaps I was inwardly guided by the views of Fr de Lubac, whose *Catholicism* had appeared in 1937. In our seminary days we had pondered, as among friends, on the intuitions of Maurice Blondel and Teilhard de Chardin, nor must I forget the openings represented, about 1937–8, by the beginnings of Catholic Action and our passionate desire for dialogue between the Church and our contemporaries.

But how were we to start a dialogue with our non-Catholic brethren? In 1942 I came to know Abbé Couturier's line of thought: an exchange of letters with him guided me to enter into the spirit of the Prayer for Unity, as he had learned it from the 17th chapter of St John. In 1945 he invited me to the first session of theology on ecumenical questions, held at St Egrève, near Grenoble. The Taizé Brothers had been living in community since Christmas, 1944: Roger Schutz and Max Thurian were among us. Can I ever forget the last day we spent with them? Together we had come to a deeper knowledge of the lesson that Unity is a mystery, whose graces we have to receive, and in which we must communicate more and more.

In the winter of 1945–6 the diocese of Valence, which bordered that in which I worked, organized monthly days of joint prayer and study for some priests and pastors. The bishop asked me to give such help with the Bible as I could offer. Today there is no need to retrace a story which opened the hearts of so many pastors to me. I believe that we loved one another sincerely, because together we bore the pain of the separations, because we prayed much together, in order to study and meditate. We never wavered in our obedience to the authorities of our Churches. There were times when this needed heroism (I simply record the fact). But I believe that the spiritual, sincere and affectionate atmosphere in which we carried on our theological dialogues made it possible for our group to survive. All the original members are now scattered to different ministries: but others took their place and though fifteen years have gone by, the group continues its work.

In 1947 Abbé Couturier invited me to join a circle of Catholic and Calvinist theologians who have met every year since 1937 in the first week of September, for a session of theological inquiry on the difficult points which seem unsurmountable to our respective Churches. It would take too long to describe the method employed, the subjects tackled, the results obtained: I hope, in the near future, to give the public the essentials of these works, as an encouragement to those who are looking for a method of interdenominational dialogue.

I have not yet spoken of the Prayer for Unity, or of what it meant to this Cevennes country, stained with the blood of Catholic and Protestant "martyrs", to discover the Week of Universal Prayer. I have always believed in the primacy of this contemplation of the mystery of Christ praying for his own. I should never have dreamt of undertaking any ecumenical task outside that spiritual atmosphere. It always hurts me when I see that the place held by this prayer is reduced, whether in theological gatherings or in public manifestations of the ecumenical task.

When Abbé Couturier died in 1953, the episcopate of France, at the instance of Cardinal Gerlier, archbishop of Lyons, decided that his work should be continued by a centre, under the name of *Unité Chrétienne*. At that time I was far from Lyons, but the Cardinal Archbishop was induced by the requests of Catholic and Protestant friends to ask my superiors to entrust me with the organization of the Centre.

That is my testimony. The facts I have briefly described show that for my part I cannot conceive that there could be a spiritual ecumenism separate from a pastoral or theological ecumenism. You know that the schema of the Council on this question asserts that spiritual ecumenism is the soul of the whole ecumenical task. Since I have been at Lyons I have come to see that it is imperative to lay down the doctrinal bases of the Prayer for Unity, as it was taught by Abbé Couturier. In fact I hold it as fundamental, whether for prayer or for theological dialogue or for any ecumenical activity, to study very carefully the following points:

1. The meaning of baptism, the sacrament of incorporation into Christ and the Church.

2. The theology of the Holy Spirit: it is not enough to affirm his place in the mystery of the Church: it is essential to emphasize the constitutive bond between the sacraments and the Holy Spirit, between the Church and the Holy Spirit.

3. In the theology of the Church, it is vital to define the relation between the local and the universal Church: this involves a number of questions, such as that of the Church as a eucharistic community.

4. There must be reflection on the eschatological dimension of the whole mystery of the Church. Especially in connection with unity, we must form a clearer idea of the tension between the "already given" and the "not yet received". This point is extremely important if we are to appreciate how the Catholic Church has a duty to pray and work for unity in the mystery of the sole will of Christ, according to the words of the eucharistic liturgy.

It is at the least in this group of ideas that it is possible to discern, gradually, the significance of the various "ecclesial communities", in themselves and in relation to one another.

These remarks imply that I consider ecumenism to be implied in any serious conception of all the Christian values and, within my Church, in a concern for the most lucid and balanced Catholic authenticity. I had never thought that it was a sufficiently restricted task to be added to others: it must be presented everywhere.

I therefore understood perfectly the reactions of several bishops and theologians of the Secretariat for Unity, who emphasized at the Council that there is no such thing as a confessional ecumenism, whether Catholic or Protestant. There are indeed Catholic or Protestant principles, in which we are steeped, for it is at the heart of our loyalties that we find dialogue, in order to advance together to the fullness of Catholicity. There again it is most important to see that the fact of the Christian divisions hinders all the Churches from expressing that fullness in the very reality of their life: and this is very definitely noted in the schema *De œcumenismo*.

At this present time it is also necessary to recall the primacy of the prayer for unity, in so far as it has to be unanimous, for it plunges us into the single intercession of Christ, so that we may cleave more totally to the mystery of his will for the Church.

The success of ecumenism depends on an ever clearer notion of the methods of work, of the end pursued, of the truth of the interdenominational dialogue. That is why I think that sessions for elementary initiation ought to be increased. On this point, it is risky to tackle special subjects too quickly, for then participants would be deprived of those first elements which are the inner illumination of the whole task.

I believe that the demands of the ecumenical spirit lead each one of us to be more deeply rooted in the mystery of the Church. My experience of more than twenty years enables me to assert that I have never known a single case of indifferentism or relativism among those who take ecumenical work seriously.

God is now inspiring vocations of consecration to the prayer for unity. Is it possible that they could be united in a new spiritual family, with a new style? Abbé Couturier thought so: in his eyes these lives, vowed to unity under a mainly contemplative form, would be the heart of the whole ecumenical task. In their present dispersion they already form, on his words, an "Invisible Monastery of Unity".

[This contribution was translated by P. J. Hepburne-Scott.]

Martin Niemoeller

Pastor Martin Niemoeller belongs to the German Evangelical Church. He was born at Lippstadt (Westphalia) in 1862. He was a naval officer and commander of a submarine during the First World War. After theological studies at Münster he became a minister of his Church in 1924. Paster Niemoeller originally wrote his contribution to this symposium in the form of a letter. In including it in this book the Editor has removed the first and last paragraphs as they contained matter unrelated to its subject-matter.

My interest in the ecumenical movement began in 1925, when Archbishop Söderblom convened the great conference at Stockholm. I was not able in those days to participate myself; but I followed the events and debates at Stockholm with great interest, since I felt that the days of a divided Christianity in our world of the twentieth century had to come to an end if the preaching of the Churches with a Christian name was to encounter confidence and trust in the non-Christian world. This interest, naturally, grew considerably during the days of the totalitarian Nazi-State in Germany when we felt very keenly that we were dependent on the prayers and intercessions of our Christian brethren all over the world. It was then that I got in touch with ecumenical organizations for the first time. During my eight years of imprisonment under Hitler I obtained my ecumenical experiences with Christian people of other denominations as well as of other nations. Thus I was "ecumenically minded" when in 1945 I came back to my family as well as to my Church. Ever since, the ecumenical movement has been my main concern.

Daniel Niles

Dr Daniel Niles was born at Jaffna, Ceylon, where he is now a Methodist minister. He did his preparatory studies for the ministry in Bangalore in South India. He preached the sermon at the assembly at Amsterdam in 1948 when the World Council of Churches was constituted. He is now general secretary of the Christian Conference of Eastern Asia.

OUR SEARCH FOR UNITY

"He that gathereth not with me scattereth."

The world is in search of "community" and unless this search is successful man looks perilously near mass suicide. At such a time, the Church is in search of "unity"; a unity which, if accomplished, would bring together the traditions of the past from many countries into a living whole, would weld together into a single fellowship persons from every class and race and nation, and would anchor humankind in true dependence on God and on one another.

The Church must succeed in her search for unity if she is to succeed in her task of serving the world. And succeed she will, for Christ has promised that the gates of hell shall not prevail against her. The only open question is whether this success of the Church will come through God's judgement overtaking the world and the Church, or whether it will come by the Church's repentance and obedience now, so that God's judgement is either averted or, if not averted, is accepted as God's call to his repentant Church to save the world by sharing its suffering. It is important that the Churches recognize that their search for unity, which is the *raison d'être* of the Ecumenical Movement, is thus a matter of life and death. "Unity" must be willed as an immediate command of God to be obeyed, rather than as a distant goal to be realized. The message of the Amsterdam assembly said:

"We intend to stay together." This resolve must be given fuller and fuller content.

But it is precisely here that the problem emerges, for the Church in different parts of the world is in a different *kairos*. The *kairos* which the Church in Ceylon faces is different, for instance, from the *kairos* faced by the Church in Britain; and yet the Churches in Ceylon are closely tied to the Churches in Britain. We, in Ceylon, feel compelled by God to seek the organic union of the Churches now. This conviction of compulsion is mediated by many factors relevant to our situation here. And when God commands us, we know that we must obey as we are able, remembering that we shall never render full and perfect obedience. All these considerations condition the way in which we meet the doctrinal problems involved in negotiating for Church union. But the doctrinal basis for a United Church in Ceylon must command the consent of our parent Churches in Britain, "the will to unity" of these Churches is at a different moment, and it is inevitable that this will condition them in expressing their judgement upon our scheme of union. But neither they nor we can or should wipe out our inter-relatedness. We belong together in one Church.

It is part of the consequence of history that God has willed that we should discover the nature of the Church by this search for the Church's unity, a method that has already made clear one fact—that the Church is not adequately defined when it has been defined purely doctrinally. The process of "becoming in history" in which the Church is involved necessarily entails non-doctrinal considerations in deciding issues about Christian unity. These non-doctrinal considerations are legitimate and inevitable, except that we must ensure that "the will to unity as an immediate command" is present in dealing with these considerations, as it must be present also in dealing with the doctrinal considerations.

But how can we ensure this? We shall ensure it by recognizing that the Church is not an end in itself. It is God's instrument in history, and the "form" of the Church must be relevant to the revolutionary forces of our time towards which it is directed. The task of the Church must take precedence in our thinking. We must also possess the humility that is the hall-mark of all wisdom. Where there is a common search for truth, there should not arise the necessity to find "face-saving" devices. It should be possible simply to say, "I now see that I have been wrong", or "that I have been partial in my understanding". A third requirement is that we should be willing to undergo the discipline which love and fellowship involve. If we had more of the urgency of love, we would not be moving at our present pace in our search for unity. Love will take risks where policy will not. How quickly ecclesiastical barriers tended to disappear at the time when enemy occupation during the war involved all in common risks and evoked from all a mutual concern! How is it that we rarely remember that the whole world is under enemy occupation? Is it because we have become reconciled to the power of Satan!

In this whole matter of the search for unity, the determining factor is simply this: Are we vividly aware of the difference between God's causes and our causes? Our causes were not always ours. They were once God's causes, now they are ours. When John Wesley met Bishop Butler, I believe that there a cause was being faced which was God's cause: when I seek to perpetuate the Methodist Church in Ceylon, because I want to preserve the Methodist tradition, then I am merely defending my cause. Let not God's light become our enlightenment, nor God's truth become our tradition, nor God's gifts become our heritage. What God has given must be at God's disposal. Israel rejected Christ because they were defending God's possessions as theirs. "He came unto his own possessions, and his own people received him not." "Come let us kill the heir", they said, "and the vineyard will be ours." There is a whole gulf of difference between the refusal to deny one's past and the refusal to put one's past at God's disposal for the future.

We must be aware of this distinction between God's causes

and our causes, not only with respect to our attitude to our several denominations, but also with respect to our attitude to other loyalties. Indeed it is even possible so to have loyalty to a particular scheme of Church union that that scheme tends to become a cause which we seek to further anyhow—our cause rather than a cause of God. This problem arises also where sometimes a denominational tradition has served the interest of a distinct class or race or nation, and where it is hard to see some alternative security for that interest. The Dutch Reformed Church in Ceylon, whose membership is almost exclusively Burgher, is a case in point. Besides, often it is not so much a question of finding alternative security as of finding a form of Church life which is congenial. The growth of the "sects" in America is a good example here. There is an "individualism" in the American way of life of which "sects" seems to be the natural Church-expression.

For all these loyalties of class, racial, national or cultural patterns, it is idle to deny that the search for Christian unity involves real danger: but the question we must determine is where God's cause lies. Is it so unthinkable that, at a time of such complete upheaval in the affairs of men, God's call to his Church to engage itself in the task of recovering Church Unity is also God's method of liberating the Church from a past that is passing away? For the problem is not simply that of denominations and the culture and social traditions in which they are rooted and to which they contribute, but rather that our whole pattern of Church life belongs to a particular milieu and that this milieu is under rapid change. What is needed is to make effective the ecumenical experience, so that a Christianity which draws its main impulse from this experience may bring to the various national and cultural streams a fresh momentum and a changed direction. The missionary movement which began in an era of colonialism has now to continue in an era of new nationalisms. Is it not natural that this change should be accomplished also by a shift away from denominationalism to ecumenism? The day is long past when, without encountering resistance, the missionary expansion of a denominationally conditioned Christianity acted also as the purveyor of national cultures. The hour has struck for the Church to recover both for itself, as for the world, that wholeness which belongs to the unity of God's creation.

But, if this change from a denominationally conditioned to an ecumenically conditioned Church life is to be achieved, it is essential that the ecumenical movement should represent a way of living together. It is not enough for it to provide a forum for conversation and debate, it should be the means of common confession of an increasingly common faith. It is not enough for it to provide an instrument of certain forms of common action; it should seek to recover the integrity of the home to which the whole family belongs. It is not enough that its method should be one of discussion only: it is necessary to create a common experience of life, for "wholeness" is determined not only by thought but also by feeling.

I have used the phrase "denominationally conditioned" in contradistinction to "denominational", for the next common step which the Churches must take in their search for unity is not so much to leave their denominationalism immediately as to accept the fact that notice has been served on them to do so. To be denominationally conditioned is to continue as if denominationalism is one's abiding home. The attitude for which this is a plea is expressed with singular simplicity in these words of a Quaker writer (Eric Hayman in *Worship and the Common Life*):

> I am writing from the point of view of some thirty years' membership of the religious Society of Friends. . . . But if this membership, and the conviction which is admittedly connected with it, have been proved through varied experience of joy and pain over this number of years, I write nonetheless as a member of the universal Church of Christ, in which alone my ultimate loyalty to him is expressed. This sense of the universal bond is so far stronger

than any denominational loyalty as to make it essential for one's most cherished ties to be tested at all times, lest they become fetters of imprisonment rather than bonds of unity in the One Spirit. Similarly, the universal loyalty binds me ever more closely to my fellow Christians in all lands, and makes it unthinkable that any conviction derived from my Christian allegiance should be magnified into a barrier of separation from a fellow Christian whose conviction, and consequent duty, may at present be opposed to my own.

The basic premise of all participation in the Ecumenical Movement is "loyalty to truth", but truth is not conveyed or unveiled by doctrinal logic alone. The truth of the Church and the truth for it lies in God's demand for "Incarnation". The Church is called to find embodiment for God's will and purpose for all his children today. He is the Shepherd of the sheep and of the wolves.

Let me conclude this article by sharing a conviction which has become ours as we have worked for Church union here in Ceylon. It is a conviction with regard to three things. First, we have come to see that the primary reality is not that we work for God but that God is working for us. "Tell David that he shall not build a house for me but that I will build a house for him." The Church is the habitation which God is building for us. We must believe the promise, "Fear not, little flock, it is your Father's good pleasure to give you the Kingdom." In the second place, we have come to see that the great temptation we must constantly watch against is the temptation to make this cause our cause. We know that if we do this we shall attempt to work for success in our own way. We know that we cannot serve God's cause unless we have the humility to take every step as God gives us guidance, and then leave the final result in God's hands. If God should say, "not David but Solomon shall build the temple", we must be willing gladly to submit. And lastly, we have come to see that there is a plain issue which we must face, the issue that we should, as individuals and as denominations, be willing to render our obedience to him. We shall never be absolutely sure that we are right in our conclusions, but all that God asks of us is the obedience of faith and not of sight. We must obey as we are able, and learn to entrust our faults to God. "I consulted not with flesh and blood", says St Paul, and that is what we also ought to do in the final issue. It is ours to render obedience. It is God's to build his house.

Bernard C. Pawley,
Canon of Ely

The Rev. Bernard C. Pawley, canon of Ely, is the official representative of the Archbishops of Canterbury and York at the Secretariat for Unity in Rome.

THE FIRST TWO SESSIONS OF THE SECOND VATICAN COUNCIL THROUGH ANGLICAN EYES

To attempt to assess the present situation of the Second Vatican Council and to forecast its eventual effectiveness would seem at present to be foolhardy. The Council is still in full spate: it has met for two sessions and the situation is very fluid. But an evaluation can be made in this way. A frequent question is posed to the Observers from other communions whether they be pessimistic or optimistic as to the outcome of the Council. The most satisfactory answer is to evade these unchristian terms and to seek to assess the present situation by comparing it realistically with the circumstances that existed only five years ago, or even with the condition of the Roman Catholic Church at the beginning of the Council.

When in 1959 Pope John XXIII of blessed memory announced that he intended to hold a Council there was great opposition to it, without doubt, from the effective government of the Church, which tried to see that as little change as possible be brought about. And there were those, equally undoubtedly, who hoped that if the preparation for the Council could be drawn out long enough, the elderly pope might not survive them and a successor without these ideas could be elected. The ultra-conservatives then in power did not believe that the Church needed doctrinal reform, since doctrine was constant. And there were no practical questions of sufficient importance, in their estimation, to warrant the summoning of this extraordinary instrument of government, a council. Thirdly, they supposed that, following the decrees of the First Vatican Council, the calling of another council might suggest that the Pope was not as unique, as sovereign or infallible as had been originally assumed.

This type of thinking reviewed from the immediate present might now well belong to the Middle Ages, such is the change that has taken place recently during the last two years. The change has not been worked out in detail nor has it been put into permanent administrative form, but its reality constitutes one of the most important single events of the twentieth century. The bishops of the Roman Catholic Church, meeting for the first time for a hundred years (and therefore in quite a different world), have decided that they, under the headship of the Pope, wish to take upon themselves the government of the Church of which they are by consecration the chief ministers.

It was realized before the Council by Englishmen that France, Belgium, Holland and parts of Germany were seething with a desire for widespread reform, but also well known was the reactionary nature of the Anglo-Irish hierarchy of the Roman Catholic Church in Britain. The whole Latin and Latin-American world was supposed to be conservative, and although some progressive spirits were recognized among the bishops of North America, the high preponderance of Irish stock was held to preclude new ideas. The situation was badly underestimated and an apology is due to those bishops throughout the world who, at first silently, had appreciated that the time for change had come.

In calling the Council Pope John gave three main directions. It was to be a bringing-up-to-date (*aggiornamento*) of the life of the Roman Catholic Church in whatever facet it was required; the pastoral needs throughout the world were to be the main consideration: and in the forefront of all minds was to be the tragic disunity of Christendom. No actual schemes for union were envisaged, but what was asked was that no one should think or speak at the Council without regard to the beliefs, aims, hopes and fears of the remainder of Christendom, called by Pope John "the separated brethren". These three aims were clearly set out by the Pope. When the prepared agenda of the Council was received by the Fathers the dismay of many men can be imagined when they saw no noticeable attempt had been made to implement these intentions. *Aggiornamento* was of the mildest kind: a recognition was made of the radio as a means of reaching the masses by conservative clerics, chosen by their bishops. There was no trace of the use of modern knowledge or restatement of the faith which was considered static: was not adaptation to meet contemporary needs a well-known heresy?

The question of unity or ecumenism was on the agenda in a form ill calculated to appeal to the understanding of those outside the Roman obedience. The old official teaching appeared once more in familiar terms. There was one Church, with one earthly head, from whom all others had separated themselves (and this included the Orthodox Patriarchates of the East). Some, for them, "difficult" doctrines must be explained again and with the removal of ignorance, prejudice and misunderstanding, the rest of Christendom would see the errors of their former ways.

When the Council met the unexpected happened. The agendas, prepared largely under the direction of prelates who had spent a lifetime in Rome, were found largely unacceptable to the bishops gathered from the four corners of the earth, and in the main unknown to each other. To the surprise of each (and to the Observers), those who objected had numerous and staunch supporters. To some the whole agenda was a plot to defeat the intentions of Pope John.

The first session of the Council therefore consisted of a determined and successful effort on the part of the bishops to wrench the power in the Church from the hands of the Curia in Rome and restore it to its original position in the corporate authority of the international episcopate, acting in conjunction with its head, the Pope. This was not so much a struggle for power as a restoration of power, the removal of an abuse of power. And with the progress of the Council so has this movement become strengthened. The magisterium, under the Pope, which the bishops have always really had, has been taken back. The concept of the Roman Curia has been superseded by the idea of a world-wide "senate" of bishops drawn from many nations and representing very wide opinions and interests. The present Pope has given these trends his personal support; and between the two sessions of the Council has himself expressed the intention of reforming the Curia.

This particular development has had widespread consequences beyond the Roman Catholic Church itself, and opened up prospects of eventual reunion. It has broken down, in the eyes of other Christians, the image of the Roman Church as an impenetrable fortress where changes were impossible. New thinking in other fields, theology, liturgy, biblical scholarship, sociology, have come under discussion which might otherwise never have gained a hearing. Ideas against which there was formerly restraint, or even persecution, have emerged; all have felt able to express opinions freely, although the Church still retains the right to declare authoritatively on these opinions.

This great freedom of discussion which has shown itself has revealed a clash (as in every free assembly) between "conservatives" and "progressives", with a less articulate, but eventually more powerful, majority sitting somewhere in the middle waiting to join one or the other. It has been the witnessing of this great event, under the guidance of the Holy Spirit, which has been the drama of the Council. It reveals a Roman Catholic Church greatly changed, and better than five years before, and a situation which will probably be the main single achievement of the Council.

The first session began with the schema on the liturgy. The bishops judged the draft by the criteria of the intentions of Pope John and none other and this united most of them. In any case the liturgical schema was probably the best yet submitted in that it had a pastoral tone; it was accepted, although it suffered considerable amendment. It has now passed into law, enabling clergy throughout the world to speak to men in their own language; and greater local freedom has been given to bishops through their regional conferences, without referring so much to Rome. The other two debates on "the two sources of Revelation" and part of the draft on "Ecumenism" were rejected as not echoing the spirit of Pope John's intentions for the Council. In between the sessions they were re-written with this spirit in mind. In this way was demonstrated the new decentralization of power in the Roman Catholic Church.

Between the sessions came the death of the beloved Pope; there were prophets who foretold that the age of reform had come to a speedy end and that the college of Cardinals would elect a successor who would return to the old pattern. But in the election of Paul VI the Roman Catholic Church found herself with the leader she needed (if the choice was to be limited to an Italian) to take up the threads of the policy dictated by his predecessor—"the Roncalli line".

The promise of the first session of the Council led to great expectations of the second, particularly on the part of the Anglican delegation. They had not been totally unprepared for the outcome, as Anglicans have always followed closely (more so than the Protestant Churches) the affairs of the Roman Catholic Church on the continent of Europe at any rate, but even to them the strength of the newly emerged party of reform was surprising. The fresh question in September 1963 was whether this Council in its new position as the Pope's advisory committee in the government of the Church would achieve revision and restatement of a radical kind.

The draft agendas rejected at the first session and due for

re-writing did not yet appear again. What to the Observers were major issues did—the Church and Unity, part II. Much Roman Catholic opinion thought that the theology of the Church needed further definition and classification. It was felt that the teaching of Pius XII on the Church as the mystical body of Christ had left some questions unanswered. The infallibility of the Pope had been defined *in vacuo* by Vatican I without setting it adequately in the context of the episcopate. The readjustment of authority in the Church necessitated some further thinking as to the exact nature of the office of a bishop. Even the classical distinction between the *ecclesia docens* (the teachers—the hierarchy) and the *ecclesia discens* (the learners—the laity) seemed to call for amendment with the growth of popular education.

Those who came to watch the Council from other confessions were most interested in the answer to the question—who is in fact a member of the Church? In Roman theology a child is made a member of Christ by baptism; what is therefore the status of someone baptized outside the Roman obedience? And following this, what was the status, as Churches, of the Christian bodies to whom these baptized people belonged? The Eastern patriarchates, such as the patriarchate of Jerusalem, had been referred to as churches, even after the separation of Rome. Such were the questions which, although they were partly ecumenical and to be considered under the heading of *De Ecumenismo*, came into the draft on the Church also.

This draft on the Church was undoubtedly a disappointment to all the Observers. The opinions of the whole body of Observers could not always be expected to be uniform and would be bound to differ. Those of the Anglican delegation could be regarded as likely to be one of the most sympathetic from first principles. Although none of them expected a rethinking of the doctrine of the Church to be carried so far by the new currents as to please entirely, it had been hoped that the draft would do more to combat non-Roman difficulties about Roman ecclesiology. (The Anglican Church believes itself with the Orthodox to have retained the Catholic doctrine of the Church, to which it considers the Roman Church to have added.) The Pope's request that the views of non-Roman Christians be taken into account, understood and answered, was ignored. The draft restated didactically the old Tridentine and Vatican formulas about the nature of the Church, with no attempt to reach a public in new circumstances. The section on the papacy, for instance, laboured the monarchical nature of this office. The texts substantiating these claims were quoted dogmatically, without showing any knowledge or reference to the volume of writing which exists questioning and examining them and showing them to be capable of other interpretation. Although no doubt the draft was not the place for controversy, some knowledge of other schools of thought should have been shown. Cardinal Bea had said that he hoped that there would be somewhere in the drafts "explanations of the dogmas which have been obstacles between us". The only explanation offered was one showing that the infallibility of the Pope (even then only under carefully defined circumstances) concerned his office, and not his person. This is already very generally understood. The problems posed by the work of such scholars as Dr Oscar Cullmann of Basle (an Observer at the Council), whose studies have threatened the biblical foundations on which the doctrine of the papacy rests, have gone unanswered. The draft evaded the question of baptism and Church membership in regard to non-Roman Christians. It was said they were "in a certain way" attached to one Church, although they were not in full receipt of the benefits of membership. The status of the other Churches outside Rome was left to the draft *De Ecumenismo*, although it was acknowledged that the Holy Spirit worked in them; and in so far as some had "valid" orders and valid sacraments, they had marks of "the true Church". The draft assumed, without question, that the Catholic Church in the Creed meant only the Church of Rome. This whole scheme was a poor foundation on which to reunite the Church of God.

The discussion which followed was, however, an improvement, since the bishops were freer to express their opinions than the drafters of the agenda, under the surveillance of the Holy Office. The principle of the "collegiality" of the bishops came out strongly and this seemed to many to be the beginning of the solution of the problems of the papacy. The conservative elements on the Theological Commission who saw this new alignment of the bishops as a threat to the papacy attacked it as theologically untenable; but they were reminded that their task was not to criticize the theology of the Council but to formulate it in intelligible theological language. The outcome therefore was hopeful for the Christian world outside the Roman obedience. The image of that Church had changed. If this picture crystallized as the result of the Council it would portray a Pope having at his call a permanent and international "senate" or subcommission of bishops, with the Roman Curia as its administrative servants; also national or regional conferences of bishops deciding which questions could properly be discussed locally and which belonged to the whole "college" of the bishops; and all this "cum Petro" rather than "sub Petro" as joint and collective heirs of the apostles. This picture of the apostolic college and succession was a familiar and welcome one to the Anglicans.

The other great source of interest to Observers in the draft *De Ecclesia* concerned the position of questions regarding the Blessed Virgin Mary. Those outside the Roman Catholic Church find in certain excessive, non-catholic devotions to Mary, not found in the Scriptures, one of the chief obstacles to union. It was interesting, therefore, to observe who would prevail at the Council, the so-called "high church" party (who wanted even further definitions of dogmas about our Lady) or the "low church" party (like Pope John) who stood for no further definitions and in fact wanted restatements to tie the existing dogmas up more closely with their foundations in Scripture and the writings of the Fathers. The outcome was interesting and satisfactory to the Observers. The inclusion of our Lady within the scope of the Church triumphant avoided the danger of sacrilege and her representation as a semi-celestial figure. It demonstrated where Mariology and Mariolatry might lead; it was said in the corridors of the Council that there were those who were "trying to excommunicate" our Lady. But the danger was averted and a genuine attempt was made to bring devotion to the Blessed Virgin Mary within the compass of the common Christian heritage.

The draft *De Ecclesia* now awaits amendment as the result of the discussions. From the Anglican point of view a very great advance has been made on the position of a few years ago. Anglicans are grateful and look forward to the following improvements which were suggested during the debate: First, that the biblical references which concern the foundation of the Church and the position of Peter among the apostles, also his relationship to subsequent bishops of Rome, will be examined carefully by those many scholars, both biblical and patristic, which the Church now has. Secondly, a knowledge of the works of non-Roman Catholic scholars in this field should be assumed and their opinions at least given some consideration. Thirdly, the existence of Churches outside the Roman communion, as Churches, must be faced, starting with the Eastern patriarchates, and drawn to its logical conclusion to consider other bodies, so that the whole issue does not appear again unresolved under *De Ecumenismo*. Fourthly, it is desirable that the place of the Holy Spirit in the Church and the preaching of the divine word be given more emphasis. It would seem to those outside her boundaries that the Roman Catholic Church has as a touchstone for others merely the existence of a "valid" ministry or sacraments, without any questioning as to whether the word of God was truly preached there or not. Fifthly, we would ask that the concept of the Church might include the image of a fellowship of sinners under judgement, yet rejoicing in God's gracious redemption. This truth shone splendidly through the opening speech of Pope Paul VI at the second session, but it was absent in the draft. The Church's glory and power were extolled continually in the Council, whereas it is known that the Church's earthly side can be sinful and fallible indeed.

The draft on Bishops and the Government of Dioceses was considered next by the Council. Much of the discussion followed upon the previous debate and was consequent upon the restoration of his ancient rights to a bishop. The powers under the revised status enable bishops to act more on their own initiative, subject to the general agreement of their colleagues in the national conferences and to the overall sovereignty of the Pope. The Anglican Observers were interested in the questioning of the practice whereby priests are consecrated to episcopal orders to fill purely diplomatic and administrative posts. This, in our eyes, was not the practice of the early Church and the removal of it would improve the image of the Roman Catholic conception of the episcopate.

The debate on Ecumenism during the second session was for the Observers of intense interest. The re-written draft gave an overall theology of ecumenism and guidance on general principles. A detailed directory of instructions for work in the field was apparently to follow. A minute analysis of the draft is impossible here. Sufficient is it to say that the new version is a considerable improvement on the original *ut omnes unum sint* which had been rejected in the autumn of 1962. It marks the official beginning of the participation of the Roman Catholic Church in the world ecumenical movement, and for this great thankfulness is felt. It is now possible to speak together (officially) without the intervention of Roman bureaucrats, and possibly to join together to say the Lord's Prayer in public without the accusation of "indifferentism"! There is a spirit of charity in the draft which is a reflection of the love which Pope John had for his "separated brethren". Many of what were held to be defects in the draft by Anglicans were pointed out by the bishops themselves during the discussions in the Council.

The first of these was what to us is considered naïve ecclesiology. Looked at carefully the conclusions were still the same: there is but one Church from which the rest of us are separated; and ecumenism means coming back to the fold (the Patriarchs of Jerusalem, Antioch and Alexandra included)! Ecumenism has therefore no real meaning. Those of us who know individual members of the Roman Catholic Church well realize that there are thinkers who see further and deeper than this and who deplore this narrow view, which is indeed itself compromised by the frank and friendly attitude in the draft towards the Oriental Churches. But in the draft lies no real tackling of this problem. The "non-orthodox" oriental Churches are referred to in the same terms as the orthodox Churches, which was perhaps not tactful; neither was the exclusion of the Anglican communion which could not allow itself to be described as a community which arose in the sixteenth century.

Here it is felt that the Roman Catholic Church must be more realistic in its ecumenical approach and appraisal of the contemporary ecclesiastical scene. It must recognize the perhaps unpalatable fact that God calls, baptizes, anoints and endows with his Holy Spirit, enlivens with his word and feeds with the holy Eucharist, in fact wholly redeems and sanctifies, Christians outside the Church of Rome. Where this is so, then there is Christ and there is his Church. The existence of an exclusive theory of the only Church in which the only true means of grace from God to man is to be found makes recognition of other communities as "churches" difficult. But it is hoped that during the third session some progress in this direction will be made in the light of one of our Lord's many rebukes to St Peter in his formative period—"what God hath cleansed, that call not thou common" (Acts 10. 15). Roman Catholics are most properly exhorted in the draft to do more to respect and understand the separated brethren who are in a certain sense members of the Church. But more than that, although it would clearly be impossible to make a general decree of communion with all the many sects, at least some attempt should be made to recognize Church status in other places on account of the evident presence of God in them.

During the debate on ecumenism there emerged the evident desire in every country except Italy to enter into dialogue. It is interesting to speculate on the point at which dialogue might start; it must eventually impinge on every facet of the Church's life. At present the problem is regarded too exclusively as dogmatic. Many Churches have sent to the Council as Observers solely professors of theology who await relaxations of doctrine on the part of Rome while they themselves sit in rigid entrenched positions. These academic discussions must take place, but they need to stay within proper proportions. Interchange of experience between congregations would be of the greatest profit. The Protestant congregation who have the discipline of listening much to the preached word would benefit from the experience of the Roman dialogue liturgy. The Catholic tradition has much to learn from the Methodist system of class teaching and so on. Anglicans in their position in the middle of a number of traditions have probably much to learn from all, and also perhaps something to teach all. From the Orthodox can be seen the meaning of faith and a picture of unity from which the rest of us can learn how we have sinned against the truth in our divisions: the Roman Catholics by adding to it and the remainder of us by taking away from it. This whole prospect is full of hope and joy for the future.

As the debate on Ecumenism came to an end there were those, especially from America, who were disappointed and felt that it was incomplete and should have included statements on the Jews and on Religious Liberty. But they were wrong, for these are highly complex questions requiring careful individual treatment. In the opinion of many Observers it was held that to include them under the general heading of ecumenism was a mistake in the first place, lest the impression be given that the Roman Catholic attitude towards those outside her own frontiers amounted merely to a general goodwill regardless of what was held, or not held, in common. The Council will eventually no doubt vote in favour of religious liberty, but they will wish to make some kind of discrimination between genuine Christian communities and the wilder new sects, particularly those who, unable to gain a hearing in their own countries, are pouring into backward areas.

The second session ended with some achievements, but with still much to do. Meanwhile the Christian world rejoices at the fresh attitudes which have emerged and looks forward to the fruits of this new spirit reflected in the projects still to be considered. The draft *De Ecumenismo* laid upon Christians everywhere the responsibility of pureness of living and evangelistic zeal as a personal contribution towards unity; all can join in the work that lies ahead and illustrate the truth that ecumenism will better be served, at any rate at the beginning, by personal example and contact, rather than by dogmatic argument.

Arthur Michael Ramsey, Archbishop of Canterbury

The Most Rev. and Rt. Hon. Arthur Michael Ramsey, Archbishop of Canterbury, was born in 1904, and has been Archbishop of Canterbury since 1961. He was previously Professor of Divinity at the University of Durham (1940), bishop of Durham (1962) and Archbishop of York (1956).

Today, as we Christian people from every part of the world and from many different traditions meet to work for unity, the supreme fact, towering above all else, is the unceasing intercession of our Lord. The seventeenth chapter of the Gospel of St John is the utterance, amid the historical crisis of the world's salvation, of a prayer which is everlasting. Our great High Priest is interceding. And for what does he pray? That his disciples may be one; that they may be sanctified; that they may be sanctified in truth. Unity, holiness, truth; as the prayer is indivisible, so the fulfilment is indivisible too. It is useless to think that we can look for unity in Christ's name unless we are looking no less for holiness in his obedience and for the realization of the truth which he has revealed.

The words of the prayer tell, however, not only of aspirations for the future, but of gifts, once for all given to the Church. By his presence in the Body of which he is the head, he has given to us already unity in himself and in the Father; he has given to us the holiness whose essence is his own self-consecration to his death upon the Cross; and he has given to us the truth which is himself, the very truth incarnate. But it is in the earthen vessels of our frailty that these gifts are ours. Never has there been a moment when the Church has not possessed the gifts, never a moment—since the friction in Jerusalem about widows or in Antioch about eating together or in Corinth about partisanship—when the Church has not obscured the gifts by the sinfulness of its members. In fulfilling its mission the Church has involved itself in the world's life, for its members have always their double citizenship of heaven and earth, their double standing as redeemed sons and members of earthly communities. Hence the Church must needs live out its unity among the changing pressures of culture and polity: it must realize its holiness amid the complexities of successive civilizations; and it must learn and teach its truth amid varieties of intellectual system and method. Small wonder that amid this involvement truth in the Church has been obscured by human sophistications, holiness has been compromised by worldly pressures, unity has been torn by these causes and many more. All the while the Church shows Christ to the world (for so great is his mercy that he uses the Church mightily despite the failure of its members), and all the while the Church tragically obscures him. But let us get our diagnosis right. Just as our mission is unity, holiness, truth, all three, so our scandal is the distortion of unity, holiness, truth, all three. No less is it in respect of all three that the call comes to our penitence, and our prayer for cleansing and renewal.

The world does not hear the call to holiness, and does not care for the truth in Christ. But the world has its own care for unity albeit conceived in a secular way: longing for peace, it desires that men and nations shall be joined to each other and the forces which separate them removed. And the world, caring thus for unity, is shocked when the Church fails to manifest it. Yet while the world's criticism must rightly humble us, we must not on that account accept the world's conception of matter. It is not just unity, togetherness with one another, that we seek; and ecclesiastics have sometimes slipped into talking as if it were, isolating unity from the other notes of the Church. It is for unity in truth and holiness that we work and pray, for that is Christ's supernatural gift to us. Let that always be made clear. A movement which concentrates on unity as an isolated concept can mislead the world and mislead us, as indeed would a movement which has the exclusive label of holiness or the exclusive label of truth.

It is when we get back to the depth and comprehensiveness of our Lord's prayer that we see that depth and comprehensiveness of our quest for unity. What does it include? It includes the ascetical, as well as the intellectual and the diplomatic and ethical. It includes the negotiation of the union of Churches and of the bringing of Churches into practical fellowship. It includes the task, within them all, of learning the truth in Christ, in Scripture, in the Fathers, in the liturgies, in contemporary scholarship, in the self-criticism of systems and formulations, a task in which we have been finding ourselves, thank God, rather less like rivals and rather more like fellow learners. It includes the doing by all of us, and where possible together, of those things which belong to our understanding of Christian conscience, so that even now Christendom may be a reality with an impact and a voice. It includes that inner consecration to Christ, in union with his Passion, whereby his holiness is wrought out in us. It includes the constant prayer of Christians everywhere, praying in which they humble themselves, praying *fiat voluntas*. All this, in depth and breadth, is what the movement to unity must be; and therefore the word "unity" does not suffice to describe it. "I believe in one, holy, Catholic, apostolic Church", and the notes of the Church are a symphony in depth telling of the depth of Christ's prayer and of the depth of its fulfilment.

Because our task is such, it has both a divine urgency and a divine patience. The call to holiness is urgent: we dare not pray, as did the unregenerate St Augustine, "Lord, give me purity, but not yet". So too is the call to unity urgent. Where there are two or three Christian bodies in a locality, the question urgently presses, "why should we not become one?" Yet just as the way of holiness cannot be hurried, and the way of truth cannot be hurried, so too there is concerning unity a divine patience. Guarding ourselves against confusing divine patience and our human sloth, we know that there is a divine patience, to be imitated in our patience with each other, in our patience with ourselves, and in our patience with God's agelong patience. Patience includes the will to see that an apparent set-back in some scheme may be our call to go into things more deeply than before. Patience includes, above all, the will to expect that God's blessing upon our cherished plans may not in his wisdom be separated from his disciplining us in holiness and in truth. We dare not forget the Psalmist's words: "It is good for me that I have been in trouble that I might learn thy statutes." And again, "Thou of very faithfulness hast caused me to be troubled." Patience is needed between those who ask that intercommunion should be immediate and general and those who, with deep conviction and no less concern for unity, think otherwise. We need to remember the moving plea made by Archbishop William Temple at Edinburgh for mutual respect of consciences on this matter.

Within the total task theology has its role. We are very conscious of the wounds which we have inflicted upon each other by our theologies, in their corruption. The West has carried to the East not only the Gospel of God, but a score of rival confessional systems which divide those who accept the Gospel; and earlier still the East had its own deadly schisms, in the fourth and fifth centuries, with tragic effects on at least two continents. Hence there is in the West today a "hand theology" spirit which says in effect, "Do not go deep in theology; we need just a few simple facts and principles in order to get unity". But those who talk thus commonly themselves make large theological assumptions which they do not pause to examine. Beware of them, for if the East cannot find unity in the confessional systems which the West brought to it in an earlier epoch, no more will it find unity in any twentieth-century simplifications. Is not the need for West and East to discover those gifts of God which authentically belong not to any one age or phase or culture or continent, but to the one Holy, Catholic, Apostolic Church of Christ, and to receive them not indeed as a return to any past age but as the media of Christ's dynamic power for the present and the future?

In the realm of theology two good things are happening. One is that within every Church theologians are being inspired by the same interests and are using the same tools. For instance, there is among Roman Catholics, Lutherans, Orthodox, Reformed, Anglicans, a kind of concern for the Bible, for the ancient Fathers, and for the liturgy which is shifting the proportions of thought and teaching and is exposing new levels for converse and partnership. The other is that within our different traditions there is a tendency to put more and more emphasis upon the mystery of God's gracious acts, bringing a deeper humility in men's view of truth and its reception. If we will be patient, true theology, good theology, is something which unites. But it will not be true unless it keeps itself and us near to the Cross whence the call to holiness comes. We need to be humbled in our contentment with our own forms of Christian culture, of intellectual method, of spirituality. We of the West shall try to learn from Asia where new chapters in Christian culture, in intellectual method, in spirituality, are yet to be written.

Unity, truth, holiness: as with the negotiator, so with the theologian his task is but a tiny fragment. All the while Christ the head of the Church goes on in his mercy using the Church, divided though it be, to make known his truth and unity and to lead many in the way of saintliness. So the divine ife of Christ's resurrection flows in a Church of which the part on earth is but a fragment as it unites us already with the glorious saints in heaven. And all the while our great high priest is interceding that in his people unity, truth and holiness may be seen.

Olivier Rousseau, O.S.B.

Olivier Rousseau is a monk of Chevetogne and editor of the ecumenical review *Irénikon.*

RETROSPECT

A visit to the Greek College in July 1921 had given me an insight into the world of the Byzantine Orient of which very little was then known. Of the great movement for Christian unity which already existed in those days less still was known.

Fr Korolevsky, who visited us on several occasions and always had something of value to communicate, revealed one day to some friends, old and young, who frequented the College of San Atanasio, that the College of San Anselmo in which we were living had been founded by Leo XIII with the idea of Eastern unity in mind. This interesting point had been completely forgotten though Dom Lambert Beauduin, who had just arrived at San Anselmo as a member of the teaching staff, paid particular attention to it. He made up his mind to tell his students about it during his course, a thing for which he was blamed. This was a subject which it was preferable not to mention. But the stone had already been cast into the sea and there was no means of stopping the waves. At all events they overflowed on to the College.

All this was during the pontificate of Benedict XV. A man of small stature but of wide vision, this pope had created around him two organisms destined, to his way of thinking, to open men's minds: the Congregation for the Eastern Church on 1 May 1917 and later, on 15 October of the same year, the Institute of Oriental Studies. Cardinal Marini, a great lover of the East and founder of the review *Bessarione*, was appointed secretary to the Congregation, the Pope reserving the presidency to himself. The Abbot of St Paul-without-the-Walls, Dom Ildefonso Schuster, future archbishop of Milan and at that time Professor of Liturgy at San Anselmo, was to assume the direction of the Institute where he organized a learned but somewhat unusual corps of professors. The new Institute passed to the Jesuits in 1921. New personalities came to join the group of these Roman unionists, such as Fr d'Herbigny, S.J., who had devoted considerable time to Russian affairs and who came to be Rector of the Institute. Moreover, the Russian emigration brought a large number of Orthodox to these parts. It was in Rome that new problems began to emerge. Generally they were solved by the classical method of missionary preparation. In this way various religious Orders founded houses with a proselytizing tendency in the regions bordering on Russia. Nothing is left of these houses today. In this cause, the Russian seminary in Lille, entrusted to the Dominicans, was founded. Though suppressed some years later, it was converted, thanks to the intelligence of its director, into the well-known *Istina* centre and transferred in 1939 to Paris where it still flourishes.

The frequent presence in Rome of the Metropolitan Szepticky, his prestige, his competence in matters relating to union, his keenness for the restoration of Slav monasticism and his exceptional broad-mindedness, attracted attention. He was rapidly given the direction of numerous projects, the most outstanding of which was the foundation in 1925 of the monastery of Amay-sur-Meuse in Belgium, transferred to Chevetogne in 1939. Under the direction of Dom Lambert Beauduin the monks sought to devote themselves body and soul to the ancient but ever-recurrent problems of Christian unity. Of these problems nothing was known, everything had to be learnt. Among the routine, conservative methods by which everything was learnt, the new group, whose organ was the review *Irénikon*, was scarcely deemed of importance. This attitude persisted for a long time but fortunately today it is a thing of the past—in June 1963 on Mount Athos on the occasion of the celebrations for the tenth centenary, the

Abbot Primate of the Benedictines, surrounded by monks of Chevetogne, affectionately embraced Patriarch Athenagoras of Constantinople.

In February 1922 Pius XI succeeded Benedict XV. The former was one of the great promoters of the movement for union during the first years of his pontificate and all we have just recorded benefited from his enthusiasm. Moreover, in the practical order, it was during his pontificate that the famous Malines conversations, centred around Cardinal Mercier, took place at the instance of Lord Halifax. The subject of much discussion at the time, they were almost always looked upon with disfavour in Rome. By a singular reversal of circumstances, we were able to hear on 3 December 1963, on the steps of the pontifical throne and only a few yards from Pope Paul VI, the great scholar Jean Guitton praising the conversations in the Council itself.

The pontificate of Benedict XV had been contemporary with the first attempts at an ecumenical movement properly so called. In 1914 the Pope had already been approached by what was later the Faith and Order movement put forward by the American Episcopalians. He was not asked for more than his support. He replied evasively but kindly. In 1918, however, *Vie et Action* was courteously suspended. The Greeks, on the other hand, proved more welcoming. This was shown in March 1919 when the young deacon Aristoclis Spiron, who is now Ecumenical Patriarch of Constantinople under the name of Athenagoras I, had just been appointed secretary to the archbishop of Athens. The latter and four other Greek Metropolitans in an important letter to the American Ecumenists manifested their real desire for the success of a "Pan-Christian" conference. The following year the Phanar put forward a more ambitious project. The events of 1922, however, which handed over the city of Constantinople to the Turks, thus destroying its newly acquired liberty, practically stopped any possible realization. In the meantime the Archimandrite Chrysostom Papadopoulos, future archbishop of Athens, set in motion a campaign to arouse the

Orthodox in favour of the great movement for unity, while the Roman Pontiff, he said, to whose prerogative belonged the supreme honour that had been offered him, persisted in his absolutism.

On the day following the second session of the Second Vatican Council an imposing number of non-Catholic observers, the majority of them Protestant or from some section of the Ecumenical Movement, and a high prelate of the Phanar, delegate of His Holiness Patriarch Athenagoras, made a similar suggestion in the presence of the Holy Father. The first echo of this was found in the extraordinary pilgrimage in which Pope and Patriarch visited Jerusalem for a few days to meet each other at the Holy Places. Today nobody would dare to reproduce the scornful and almost degrading terms with which even the best of the Catholic press stigmatized the earlier Orthodox gesture. Today thousands of pilgrims are united around the ecclesiastical leaders.

The fortune of the expressions "Pan-Christian", "Pan-Christianity", was not, indeed, a happy one. Nothing is more natural on the lips of a Greek than to use the word "pan" to express every universalist tendency, and in Western languages nothing is more natural than for it to have a slightly pejorative flavour. These movements also unleashed endless suspicion in excessively vigilant and more or less ill-informed circles. The international conferences of *Faith and Order*, like those of *Vie et Action*, were interpreted as a lack of recognition of the differences between confessions and were judged dangerous. In 1928, under the pressure of urgent requests, Pius XI decided to publish his encyclical *Mortalium animos*, condemning these movements. Even today those two sinister words make ecumenists of all confessions tremble. For the future, Pius XI, somewhat discouraged, showed in his attitude and actions a preference for the missionary movement.

The review *Irénikon*, which was thought to be included in the condemnation, lost almost five hundred subscriptions overnight. Rome let us know later that the encyclical did not condemn us, but this was something we could not put before the public. Moreover, they would not have believed us. (It is interesting to note that immediately after the announcement that a Council was to be convoked the review amply recovered from this set-back.) Dom Beauduin, however, who had taken part in the Malines Conversations and who, after the death of Cardinal Mercier in 1926, had become the scapegoat for all the animosity and disapproval, had to abandon his foundation and remain in exile for twenty-two years.

Perhaps I may be allowed to relate here a short personal experience. In 1929, when I was in the monastery in which I was professed (Maredsous: I was unable to rejoin Amay until 1930), for a few days I had to accompany two young Italian priests who were on a visit to the North for the purposes of study. They were particularly interested in the liturgy and had come to Amay from Maria-Laach. The older, Graziolo, Church History Professor in a Lombardy seminary, was also interested in the movement for Christian unity and both had heard of the difficulties of the Amay foundation immediately after the encyclical *Mortalium animos*. It was difficult to make them understand that all was not ended and that the wick was still smoking. I have often thought, in recalling this conversation, of the pilgrims of Emmaus, but at that time it was with difficulty that I succeeded in convincing them. Now the younger of the two—he was then thirty-two—was John Baptist Montini. In 1964, as Paul VI, he praised in an allocution the liturgical and ecumenical work of the Belgian monasteries.

The lack of open-minded sympathy for ecumenism at this time was calculated to discourage the Protestant and Orthodox world so far as a working relationship with Rome was concerned. There was uniate proselytism, individual conversions, ecumenism, a spirit of "retaliation" and an attempt to smile on the one hand and frown on the other. Dom Beauduin's chief merit lay precisely in his having seen in a flash that this was a mistake, but this intuition cost him dear. Surely we are all united in a certain manner with Christ in our baptism? *Quod Deus conjunxit, homo non separet.* Cardinal Bea has repeated this continually in his teaching in recent years. This is again, quite certainly, a new victory.

In 1927 the Amay monastery was linked with the *Pro Russia* Commission. This, being independent of the Congregation for the Eastern Church, demanded in 1930 that our work programme should follow its own direction and be limited exclusively to Russia. Nothing was said to us of the problem of unity. *Irénikon* was thrice suppressed by Rome. Another title, *Russia of Yesterday and Tomorrow*, was suggested to us. Exchanges of telegrams ended in the withdrawal of these measures and nothing of them was heard in the outside world. Something graver now happened—Amay itself was suppressed in 1931. We only learnt this six months later when all had already been re-established; it had not been thought necessary to inform us.

In 1935, the *Pro Russia* Commission was attached to another monastery and we heard no more of it. The Congregation for the Eastern Church demanded its rights. This was under the kindly and understanding rule of Cardinal Tisserant. Today, in the Council, Russian observers from the Patriarchate of Moscow rub shoulders with Anglicans, Lutherans, Baptists and other Nonconformists. Under this aspect of things, the exclusiveness already proposed was seen to be an obstacle and the Secretariat for Union, under the formal orders of John XXIII, had to assume among its other responsibilities contacts with the Orthodox world, since the Commission for the Orient declared itself incapable of making them.

Gradually the anti-ecumenical bias weakened, though a strong arm was necessary to give it a complete change of front. A year after the famous Assembly of Amsterdam, when the World Council of Churches was finally established, an instruction from the Holy Office authorized—even encouraged—the bishops of the world to open the door to ecumenism and, moreover, with numerous recommendations, invited the faithful to inter-confessional meetings at which the

Lord's Prayer—the prayer of forgiveness—would be recited in common. This certainly constituted a tremendous step forward. As one of my brethren, a veteran fighter for unity, then pointed out to me, "This is the result of twenty-five years of hidden, laborious, energetic and constant efforts on the part of those in the Catholic world who have devoted themselves body and soul to our cause".

A little later, thanks to the initiative of two excellent Dutch priests, well known today, Mgr Willebrands and Fr Thijssen, the "Catholic Conference for Ecumenical Problems" was founded—the forerunner of the Secretariat for Christian Unity. The latter at once brought a considerable change to relations with other confessions, and prepared the way, with complete success, for the presence of observers at the Council, one of the things John XXIII most desired.

Numerous visitors soon came to frequent the small monastery of Amay. (I apologize for speaking of it again, but my best memories are there.) Among them were Lord Halifax, long since dead, who had he lived would have seen the realization of his dream—a meeting face to face between the Archbishop of Canterbury and the Holy Father.

Today it is fashionable to be ecumenical but then it was daring and one had to resign oneself to a certain amount of abuse. But now the censures have been transformed into applause. It is the law of life. Almost all the bishops during the Council have spoken in favour of ecumenism. Doubtless, as Fr Congar recently wrote, "there is no question of the bishops putting their hands to the task in a common will to work for unity". Contrary, however, to what was expected, the Council has declared itself with a surprising majority "positively favourable". The recalcitrants are increasingly rare and form the small, dissatisfied group which is fighting against the *aggiornamento* and the Council, denouncing the evil wrought thereby that "fifty years will not be sufficient to put right".

In its recent chronicle of the Council, *Informations Catholiques* quoted the following remark by a well-known theologian: "Who would have thought, two years ago, that having regard to the general atmosphere which obtained in the Catholic Church before the Council, we were going to find a majority of votes favourable to the proposals of the Secretariat for Christian Unity, which in actual fact are very bold?" New horizons and a greater deepening of our ecclesiology, decentralization, a liturgical life better lived, constant efforts towards unity—all this was precisely what we were aspiring to forty years ago. What has happened in recent months has shown that we were pursuing an aim that was good.

We have even seen Pope Paul VI visit the Holy Land where he met Patriarch Athenagoras. On the occasion of another pilgrimage to Jerusalem in 1959, Patriarch Athenagoras declared, "I take advantage of my pilgrimage to launch an appeal to all the religious leaders of the Christian communities on the question of the union of the two Churches, Orthodox and Catholic. I invite all the members of the clergy of this city to work for the realization of this union, above all here where our Saviour called us to love, peace and unity. The Christians of the whole world have their eyes fixed on their brothers of this eternal city where Christ appeared and began his mission. Charity, peace, union, the threefold recommendation pronounced by our Saviour which we ought all to realize in the present circumstances." Was not this a prophecy on the part of the Patriarch who, a few months earlier, had called John XXIII a true precursor, "There was a man sent from God whose name was John"?

[This contribution was translated by Kathleen Pond.]

Edmund Schlink

Edmund Schlink was born in Darmstadt in 1903 and is a member of the German Evangelical Church. He studied at Würtemberg, Munich, Kiel and Vienna, was ordained in 1931 and became Professor of Dogmatic Theology at the University of Heidelberg in 1947. He founded the Ecumenical Institute in the university. He is an observer at the Council as a member of the World Council of Churches.

WILL THE SEPARATION OF THE CHURCHES BE OVERCOME?

The separation of the Churches can only be overcome through a revolution in the fundamental suppositions on a basis of which the joint theological discussions of the separate Churches are at present being undertaken. I am thinking now not only of the German Reformed Church and the Roman Church, but more especially of the many different Churches in the world with their various traditions. The mutual opening up of these separate traditions can only be achieved through some explosive event that will burst like a storm in the hearts of men.

All these traditions are contained in Jesus Christ, both the Christ who has already come and the one who is to come. He came as the friend of sinners and the enemy of Pharisees and those learned in the Scriptures. He will come as the Judge, not only of the world but also of the Church—see for example the message of the Apocalypse—this is common knowledge. The first step towards the unification of the Church will be when we not only know this, but when we are all moved to the depth of our hearts and accept the fact that the Lord of the Church makes us all radicals and doubters. Then we shall no longer pride ourselves on the history of our Church and its decisions, and face divine justice assured of their certainty, but we shall devote ourselves to penitence, which will show us that the life of our Church, its doctrines and its institutions only partially correspond to the fullness of the Kingdom of God in Christ. Let us not seek in our penitence to justify and defend ourselves against other Churches, but let us, together with them, see ourselves and our need for grace, and in view of that need let us seek no longer to point out the defects in other Churches but rather to participate in whatever God has confided to them.

Thus, in addition to bringing some transparency to the partitions dividing the Churches, we shall make known the secret of the body of Christ—that is, Christ ever present and active, through the Holy Ghost, is more magnificent, more merciful and more understanding than we believed. Let there be no doubt that our divisions obscure and disfigure the mysterious unity of the Body of Christ, but they cannot destroy it.

It is this understanding of the Church through the separated Churches that is the supposition necessary for the unification of the divisions. Unification will no longer be sought through the subjection and absorption of the other Churches, but will gradually emerge as the result of a mutual relaxing of barriers between the whole community. Naturally, this cannot take place without exchanges on the part of the participants. These exchanges, however, should not be seen as a sacrifice but as the acquisition of wealth.

Are these suggestions merely postulates? No, because this soul-searching has already begun with the ecumenical movement and is becoming more and more widespread. Is this excessive zeal? No, not if one accepts the real significance of the basis common to all, which is apostolic in its oneness throughout history. But with this condition, are we not stating once more the whole problem of Scripture and tradition?

The ecumenical movement has not been initiated for the sake of a principle of Scripture or for a joint determination of the relationship between Scripture and Tradition. But in the combined theological work and in the common spiritual life of the Churches of the World Council, the Bible has once again become the basis common to all, not that this enables ecclesiastical traditions to be left aside, but because the latter are to be understood more and more as an historical development of the wealth of the apostolic basis, and consequently also as the common heritage of God's people on earth. Seen in this way, many of the arguments that previously seemed important have lost their significance.

[This contribution was translated by A. F. Price.]

Cardinal Léon Joseph Suenens

Cardinal Léon Joseph Suenens, Archbishop of Malines-Brussels, was born in 1904, ordained in 1927, and became Professor of Philosophy at Malines seminary in 1930. He was made auxiliary bishop of Malines in 1945 and succeeded Cardinal van Roey as Archbishop of Malines-Brussels in 1961. He was created cardinal by John XXIII in 1962. He is the author of many books, several of which have been translated into English (*Christian Life Day by Day* [1964], and *The Nun in the World* [1964], etc.).

THE ECUMENICAL MOVEMENT TODAY

The Catholic ecumenical movement as it exists today takes its major direction from the contemporary mind of the papacy, of which the dominant note was struck by Paul VI in his coronation allocution:

> Here it is moving to contemplate the inheritance from our unforgettable predecessor Pope John XXIII who, under the inspiration of the Spirit, called forth such great hopes which it is our honour and duty to pursue.
>
> It is true that, no more than he did, we cherish no illusions on the scope of the problem to be resolved and the gravity of the obstacles to be surmounted. But, true to the instruction of the great apostle whose name we have taken, *Veritatem facientes in caritate* (Eph. 4. 15), we undertake to pursue, depending only on these means of truth and charity, the dialogue which has been entered upon. and to advance the work which has been degunto the best of our ability. (*Documentation Catholique*, 21 July 1963, c. 934.)

"To pursue the dialogue which has been entered upon and to advance the work which has been begun"—that is indeed the principal purpose of the Catholic ecumenical movement at the present time.

The dialogue has been most positively engaged by the setting up of the Secretariat for Christian Unity. This was not of course a novel idea. On 19 March 1895, Leo XIII had established a *Commissio pontificia ad reconciliationem dissidentium cum Ecclesia fovendam* (A.A.S., vol. 28 (1895), p. 323); but its existence was only short-lived. The Secretariat for Christian Unity, established by John XXIII on 5 June 1960, would appear to correspond better to hopes throughout the Church, which recognized at once the undoubtedly profound significance in the life and structure of the Catholic Church of a form of official organ commissioned with the dialogue between separated Christians.

This dialogue entered an historic stage during the first session of the Second Vatican Council. This was first and foremost through the presence of the forty non-Catholic "observers". After spending a week in familiarizing themselves with all the ins and outs of the Council organization, they started to converse with a number of sympathetic bishops, and then with others, desiring thereby to be acquainted much more personally with the representatives of those whom they only knew very indirectly in their dioceses. This activity grew and spread; conversations, receptions, less formal meetings wove what might be called a close web of ecumenical relations. That in itself is surely already one real achievement of the Council.

But in most of their contributions the Fathers, too, showed that a dialogue had been entered into. A sufficient example is their insistence that the schemata should bear more impress of an ecumenical spirit. Many of their addresses formed what was in fact doctrinal dialogue with their interlocutors, themselves indeed silent on the occasion but whose voices and views were thereby publicly expressed. The result is that the schemata will be impressed by ecumenical thought and will stand as a fact among future generations, as an existing sign and a call to continue progress.

For this, too, is one of the ecumenical notes of Paul VI's pontificate: "to advance the work which has been begun".

This entails the advancement of mutual knowledge. So many misunderstandings derive from the fact that separated Christians know each other little, are uninformed about each other's spiritual life and forms of piety, works of charity and relief, missionary zeal and the enormous sacrifices made for the missions. In the same way, the causes of the divisions, the intentions of their leaders, the divers fortunes of these most unhappy separations are known only in their barest outlines.

Christians, then, must come together. In an age which has come to think in terms of one world, and in which even the most opposed of men succeed in restraining their hostility in order to pursue certain human aims together, it is inconceivable that Christians, with their religious objects, should not meet to explore the causes of their disagreements and find remedies, so that the distinctive marks of the Christian religion, charity and peace, may shine forth the more.

We must increase practical collaboration, especially in the field of social and human welfare: problems of world hunger, epidemics and national disasters, population and housing, illiteracy, the distribution of material good things, and so on. In these days when one and all follow striking world events, the disciples of Christ by their very calling, and without glossing over their differences, must plan and work together to support all forms of aid and relief.

We must also increase heartfelt prayer in common. We speak of this last because of the particular delicacy of the question; prayer in common is at once a nourishment of unity and its plainest witness. But common "spiritual approach" to the "problems" of ecumenism is obviously necessary. The 1949 Instruction of the Holy Office, *Ecclesia Catholica*, declared in its Introduction that it is the Holy Spirit who is at work in this movement towards unity which is quickening all disciples of Christ. There is to be remembered, also, the wide recognition that the Week of

Prayer for Christian Unity every January has won for itself. The question of unity is a problem of the Church which first and foremost must be realized on its fundamental, theological level, as pertaining to the life of the Father and the Son breathing in the Spirit.

"We cherish no illusions on the scope of the problem to be resolved and the gravity of the obstacles to be surmounted", said Pope Paul.

The problem is great enough. We have only to look at facts and figures. There are some nine hundred million Christians, of whom a half are Roman Catholic; this, when Christ, the founder of Christianity, prayed on the eve of his death "that they may all be one; that they too may be one in us, as thou, Father, art in me, and I in thee" (John 17. 21). On top of this, Christians are face to face with two thousand million non-Christians, to whom they, in a state of division and even discord, offer a religion which they proclaim to be the religion of charity: "The mark by which all men will know you for my disciples will be the love you bear one another" (John 13. 35). This is the outward aspect but also perhaps the greatest scandal of the situation.

The problem is as vast in its inner nature, since those differences inhering in the Christian Churches themselves make it so difficult to come together. There are dogmatic differences; those which run through the reports of the "Faith and Order" Conferences at Lausanne (1927), Edinburgh (1937) and Lund (1952), not to speak of that which has just taken place at Montreal (1963), show clearly the doctrinal disagreements which exist between bodies which are themselves members of the World Council of Churches. Among non-theological difficulties are social and cultural factors which are often in fact decisive; these may be seen in the manner in which history teaching presents the origin and present state of separated Churches, the identification which became established of certain Churches with certain nations, the fact that Churches have emphasized their differences down the centuries, thus confirming their separation, the weight of institutions and organizations which often strengthen and concentrate divergences, the human tendency to accept the *status quo*—and so on.

This being so, the best service which Catholics can render ecumenism is to begin by renewing themselves in the Spirit and the Gospel that they may present to non-Catholics a Church whose features, above all in their doctrinal and essential proportions, are as perfect as is possible, which is to say as faithful as possible to the will of the Lord. There are real dogmatic differences; but they may be intensified by the theology which expounds them, the style of the arguments which support them, and the manner in which they are expressed in the systems and life of the Church. These are indeed "accidentals", but their consequences are considerable. There are inviolable necessities in the constitution of the unity of the Church; but it is possible also in the name of that unity practically to impose more or less consciously on "the others"—under penalty of remaining outside the Catholic Church—ideas, forms of spirituality, practical customs, in short a way of life and a set of demands, which do not belong to the essentials of Catholic unity.

In accomplishing this renewal, Catholics will be directly responding to a purpose of the Second Vatican Council. We know John XXIII's intentions in convoking it. He said that we have to undertake a re-appraisal—*aggiornamento*—a spiritual renewal and fresh spring of vigour in the Church, that she may be seen in all her beauty; then, when we have accomplished this complex task, removing everything that, humanly speaking, forms an obstacle to unimpeded advancement, we will present the Church in her splendour, *sine macula et sine ruga* (see the *Osservatore Romano*, 10-11 August 1959, and *Documentation Catholique*, 6 September 1959, c. 1099). It is clear from this that in one of its main objectives the Second Vatican Council is explicitly ecumenical.

It is, moreover, to the whole Christian community that this urgent call is addressed. Separated Christians are not looking for this spiritual renewal, a holy countenance, the doctrinal and essential proportions, in books or records, nor only in the schemata of the Second Vatican Council, but in the community of all the faithful as it exists, in its thinking, prayer and way of life. It is among Catholics as a whole and individually, through their spirituality, ideas and attitudes, that the Reformed Churches and the Orthodox may be said to meet Catholicism. It is Catholics as a whole and individually, in all that they are and do, who compose the characteristic features of the Church as they are seen by our separated brethren. In short, even as we derive our view of Lutheranism from practical observation as well as its Confessions of Faith, so Protestants form their opinions of Catholicism from what they see of members of the Catholic community. In an age of ecumenism every conscientious Catholic bears a heavy responsibility, he personally involves the whole Church.

As for the future of ecumenism, so far as a human estimate goes, we must not "cherish illusions" as if actual union was a thing of tomorrow. "First the drawing together, then the meeting, and finally perfect reunion" is how John XXIII expressed it (*A.A.S.*, vol. 51 [1959], p. 380; *Documentation Catholique*, 4 September 1960, c. 1101). We are still at the stage of drawing together, with some meetings. The Catholic Church's corporate ecumenical work is comparatively recent; it is developing by leaps and bounds, but that does not mean that we human beings are in any position to foretell the future. A separation of so many centuries, especially when it is a question of religious institutions, leaves a deep imprint which will not be soon effaced. The drawing together of Churches will necessitate considerable re-appraisals, indeed, and real changes in men and structural organization, but at a slow and measured, sometimes even uncertain pace. If there is great toil in stirring up the Christian people so that they may be in a "state of mission", it is equally arduous to engage the Church as a whole in an age of ecumenism.

It is for each of us to sow: others perhaps will reap—the Gospel saying is always true. It is for each of us also to consider what particular task is asked of him; the position in the dioceses in Europe, let alone in Asia, Africa and America, is so diverse that ecumenical work must carefully observe the indications given by the local hierarchy. Each must devote himself faithfully to that mission which the Lord entrusts to him in this field of labour: there is he who has authority in the community and gives it leadership; there is he who prays, uniting himself to the Lord's prayer for unity (John 17); there is he who is a student of ecumenism and communicates the fruit of his studies: there is he who is suffering and who offers for unity that sharing in the Passion of the Saviour. It is the bounteous Lord himself who will sustain to its consummation that work whose first steps he has inspired and whose first fruits he has ripened.

[This contribution was translated by Rachel Attwater.]

The Taizé Community

The Community of Taizé, the first Protestant monastic community since the Reformation, was founded at the beginning of 1940. Roger Schutz, a student of theology at Lausanne, decided, in 1939, to form a group of a few friends to work together inspired by communal prayer, and organized lectures and spiritual retreats for them. In August 1940 he bought a large unoccupied building in the city of Taizé near Cluny and, on account of the war, established himself there.

In 1942 he was joined by the first three brothers, amongst them, Max Thurian. For two years they lived in Geneva and later, after the liberation of France, moved into Taizé. In these first years the essential principles of the community were established. Later, three new brothers entered Taizé. These seven original brethren took their vows at Easter in 1949. This was a decisive stage, as it consecrated the monastic character of the community. Each brother promised complete celibacy, renunciation of all property and obedience.

At present the community has more than sixty brethren, drawn from some ten different countries in Europe and the New World and from many of the Reformed Churches (from such varied origins as the Lutheran, Calvinist and Episcopalian traditions). Because of this international and interconfessional character, Taizé is a symbol of unity at the heart of world Protestantism. But the unity for which the community is now working has a much wider implication, namely the visible unity of all Christians, upon which the unity of all men depends.

Ecumenical contacts are part of the daily life of the community, either at Taizé (visitors, pilgrims who come to pray in the church of Reconciliation, symposium of Catholic bishops and pastors, etc.) or elsewhere through the travels of the prior or the brethren that he appoints for this work. Since 1949 the prior, accompanied by Brother Max, has paid frequent visits to Rome, gaining more and more friends in many different ways. They have often been received by Popes Pius XII, John XXIII and Paul VI. They have both been invited by the Secretary for unity to be observers at the Council.

Since the Council has been in progress other brothers have also gone to Rome, in order to put into practice immediately the same work of prayer and hospitality as at Taizé.

Contact with the Orthodox Church has been likewise increased, and an Orthodox Centre, a dependant of the Patriarchate of Jerusalem, is being built on the hill at Taizé, next to the church of Reconciliation. The ties with the World Council of Churches at Geneva and with the French Protestant Federation in Paris are evidence of the sincere desire for a free exchange of ideas on the part of all Christian brethren.

THE VATICAN COUNCIL AND THE POWER OF PATIENCE

The year 1963 was historic because during its course two events in the Christian world transcended all the denominational frontiers to affect men of the most divergent beliefs and ideologies.

The first of these was the Encyclical *Pacem in Terris*, a most lucid document written in simple language. John XXIII, wishing to make a pronouncement which would concern everybody, took the decision to issue this encyclical after a night of conversation and meditation with God—as he himself used to call it. This causes one to reflect on the way in which God makes his will felt in one of the oldest institutions in the world.

The second was the death of John XXIII, which for several days held the attention of believers and non-believers throughout the world. His death brought confirmation to even the most sceptical that his words were in perfect harmony with his inner Christian life.

It was impossible not to bear in mind these two events during the second session of the Council, and thus the figure of John XXIII continued to dominate, closely identified with that of his successor, whose intention unquestionably is to continue the same policy.

Bearing in mind our own introspective attitudes and the constant introversion of our Christian societies, which are incapable of influencing the non-Christian groups that are daily becoming more important, it is impossible to ignore these two events—unique in the history of our times—in which Christian faith and thought have had universal repercussion.

Hope sustained by struggle

Together with nearly all the fathers of the Church at the Council beneath the dome of St Peter's, I, as an invited observer, experienced daily a sort of deep interior struggle which, for me, took place on two fronts at the same time.

Firstly I asked myself about the Council—as doubtless many others—whether John XXIII's aims which had been taken up by Paul VI would be achieved and whether the Council was going steadily ahead towards its essential aims, or if, on the contrary, it was wasting time in discussions of secondary importance. The question uppermost in my mind was this: Will the Council succeed in finding a means of drawing nearer and of ministering to that great body of unbaptized people who have broken all links with their faith? Indeed, I remain convinced that the Council will be a success if it finds an answer to this great and grave problem of our days. At the present moment the Council is making progress. It is quite natural that it should have awakened hopes; but these hopes have nothing euphoric about them: they can only be sustained by daily struggle.

I have said however that this interior struggle of mine took place on another front as well. This great meeting which is the Council demanded that the Fathers attending it should break their silence to question one another. This is an essential part of any meeting and, in family circles when brothers have kept apart from each other, there comes a moment when they must re-appraise one another by means of a conversation at times hurtful and searching. This is a painful process for those brothers who make an effort to love one another, and when one member suffers all suffer with him. In this way the Council is a test of a purifying nature if, instead of being rejected outright or merely frigidly consented to, it is accepted wholeheartedly by us.

The Second Vatican Council proceeds by stages

Since the end of the second session pessimistic rumours have been circulating about the Council work and some people feel disillusioned. But it is imperative to understand that in order to achieve its goal, that of adapting and translating the universal message for our times, the ground had first to be smoothed and many questions appearing to have no visible connection with the objective have to be tackled. Among many others, three main themes have been the subject of much thought.

The Council had considered the theology of the episcopate, causing the bishops themselves to go to the sources of a doctrine which needs to be reconsidered with the aim of reinspiring the local churches and the dioceses whose guiding force *par excellence* is the bishop.

Again, when considering the theme of the holiness of the Church the Council deliberated on the very important subject of the spiritual life; such a theme was by no means easy to bring into the open in the Council gathering. We have repeatedly heard that sanctity is a call addressed to every Christian and that the sanctity of the faithful sustains those of the Church and that, conversely, it enables everyone—members of the hierarchy, priests, faithful and religious—to realize that they are all servants one of the other. Everyone was on his guard against the temptation to exercise his privileges over his brother and to impose, more or less deliberately, his demands on his neighbours.

Finally, the Council examined the Ecumenical Movement, a subject which forms an integral part of the great search for a pastoral method for all people; up to a certain point it is true that the spread of the Gospel is closely bound up with ecumenism, that one is impossible without the other and that in order to affect people of the present day (and here lies the main problem), we must present a united front. We assert, in fact, as a part of our faith that the unity of all people must be achieved through the unity of the Church or otherwise it will never come about.

Some are frightened by all that ecumenism entails and it cannot be denied that dangers exist in this field as in all others. But what we must always bear in mind are God's promises to us at the end of our journey. The immeasurable benefit of our visible unity will have to be bought at the price of the possible mental confusion of a few.

A first balance sheet

Theology of the episcopate, spiritual development of God's people, ecumenism, there are the main headings, but its real concern is with the present-day world. And so, before considering this, which should be one of the dominant themes of the next session, the Church had to ask itself—"What is your opinion of yourself?" The man of today, be he Catholic, Orthodox or Protestant, who feels himself appealed to daily by a world unable to share in the hope offered by Christianity, expects the Council to deal with the problem of the Catholic Church's place in the world.

In Rome together with my brethren, seated daily at the same table with bishops and cardinals, we have found that unparalleled progress has been made. If today the Council were unexpectedly to be interrupted one of its major achievements would remain established, bringing a new spirit into the majority of Catholic dioceses. Often I have heard bishops using such phrases as: "As we leave we are no longer the same as when we arrived" or "The Council has caused a personal conversion in me which I must transmit to my diocese". They also expressed their intention of living in the spirit of poverty of the Beatitudes and of being servants before all else. One may therefore expect a transformation in certain dioceses.

The impulse of the first session was due in part to the fact that bishops from all countries were getting to know each other. It was not just a matter of 700 bishops, almost all European, as in the First Vatican Council, but of 2,300 bishops from all parts of the world meeting and talking with one another.

The impulse of the second session seemed less, but in actual fact it penetrated far deeper below the surface and hence produced less visible results.

This inner driving force is not maintained merely by simple impulses, and we must remember that they are not sufficient by themselves unless backed up by a driving force inspired by the deepest theological thinking. There is a certain very necessary power in being patient, since it is just that which prepared the minds of those people of restless and inquiring faith during the past years for what we are now able to discern in the work of the Council.

ROGER SCHUTZ.

[The above was translated by P. Fussell.]

THE SECOND VATICAN COUNCIL AND ECUMENISM

When, on 25 January 1959, Pope John XXIII announced the calling of the Council, the world saw it as a Council directly concerned with the union of separated Christians. This was speedily contradicted by the indication that the Roman Catholic Church was first dedicated to the resolving of internal problems before contemplating a Council for union. After the first two sessions, however, it was clear that the idea of Christian unity was playing a great part in the debates and written texts. The importance of the presence of observers at the Council meetings can hardly be exaggerated. Though they took no active part in the discussions, their very presence was a sign and a clear call to the Fathers. When they were dealing with more specifically Roman Catholic concerns, and necessarily when they had questions of Christian unity in mind, they could not but address themselves to all baptized Christians. Indeed it became habitual with many of the Fathers to direct their addresses not only to the *eminentissimi ac reverendissimi Patres* but also to the *carissimi Observatores* (and in the second session to the lay auditors also). This was not just a polite formula; we could feel the real desire to be heard and comprehended by non-Roman Christians.

Thus it was that the Council, taken to be a Council to prepare for unity, in spite of denials did in fact stand revealed as in fact what the world had in part thought, and assuredly according to the concept which sprang from the mind of good Pope John. It is not indeed a Council for union; but it is all the same a Council of preparation for the visible unity of Christians. How is this so, and in what way can it achieve its end? What are the problems it raises in the remaking of Christian unity, the solutions which it may propose and the obstacles presented on the way?

Reform of the Church

The Roman Catholic Church undertakes a reformation

Ten years ago it would have been rather daring to talk or write of the reformation of the Church. With the Council, Pope John XXIII expressed the idea of *aggiornamento* in the Church, an idea which entails a bringing up to date. This means on the one hand that the Church feels herself to have grown old in certain of her institutions and aspects, and desires to submit herself to a rejuvenation under the power of the Spirit. Her message is not reaching out to modern man, and she must bring her pastoral practice back into focus, as it were. One of the purposes of the Council is pastoral; that is to say, the Church is seeking a new and fresh expression of eternal truth which will correspond with the needs and language of the modern world. But, on the other hand, *aggiornamento* also signifies that the Church desires to revitalize her message through communication with the sources of faith. The simple pastoral *aggiornamento*, to correspond with modern man, leads the Church to a theological *aggiornamento* to correspond with God's will for our times. Doctrine and pastoral practice are bound up together and one cannot be "brought into focus" without the other. It is true of course that in the Council the Roman Catholic Church has no intention of making alteration in her dogma. But doctrines are susceptible of interpretation, and if the Church in her pastoral labours seeks to be better understood by modern man, then in her theological work she is brought to rethink the expression of her dogmas, in order to inspire that pastoral work which is aimed at leading contemporary men to witness to Christian truth in the whole of their lives. For the Church, to rethink the expression of her dogma is to renew her thought and language at the very sources of faith: the Scriptures, apostolic tradition, the living liturgy and, essentially, in the charity of Christ.

All this is good, and a real reform of the Church—not a change of fundamental doctrines, but the endeavour to revitalize the Church's message from the sources of faith and in view of modern man. Such a reforming endeavour can only be in favour of the visible unity of Christians. Schism has often been produced through the Church's refusal to accept a necessary reform or through tardiness therein. Looking back, we can say that if the reformation brought about by the Council of Trent had been achieved at the beginning of the sixteenth century there probably would not have been the Protestant Reformation, while the Catholic reformation would not have had to take its stand in an attitude of opposition to schism. We cannot of course remake history; all share the responsibility for different wrongs, and schism is never desirable or beneficial. We can, however, rejoice that the Catholic Church today is courageously facing a reformation whose consequences may be far-reaching. It is to be hoped that the non-Catholic Churches will also undertake this reforming endeavour, for they are often frozen into their institutions. It is only such a universal reform throughout the Christian world that can prepare the way for the visible unity of Christians in one Church.

The Church's desire to be the Poor Servant

The Council has witnessed a fresh stirring of the vocation of poverty in the mind of the Church. There has been mention of the "Church of the poor", though here of course there is an inaccuracy as the Church is everyone's Church. Gradually, however, the idea was clarified, and it was realized that the intention of many bishops was to restore the life of the Church to the state of service and poverty.

The Church, and especially the hierarchy, is often described juridically, in terms of prerogatives and authority. Today the need is felt everywhere for a return to a more biblical and humble manner of expressing the Church and her ministry. Without entirely abandoning the juridical aspect of the Church, there is the wish to see the concept of charism (the gift of the Holy Spirit) replace that of prerogative, and the concept of "diaconate" (service of the people of God) that of authority. These two biblical concepts of the gift and of service imply the virtue of poverty. The Church knows that she is nothing without the power of Christ and the gifts of the Spirit; she waits as it were with hands outstretched to be given all things by the Father. At the same time, what she has thus received in her poverty she cannot keep to herself, for her own glorification and well-being, she must loose it free in order to transmit it to the world, to give it to all men, for she is the servant of all. From the first session of the Council there have been condemnations of "triumphalism", that pleasure in the contest, in victory and fame, which is a temptation for the Church. The idea of the Church as the poor servant provides the positive aspect of the triumphalist criticism which is in itself only a negative.

The debate on the schema concerning the Virgin Mary had the same implications, and in a way symbolized the Church's conciliating direction of thought. Perhaps in succession to a period in which the Roman Catholic Church has believed it necessary to emphasize the greatness of Mary's vocation, is coming a time when it is needful to emphasize her poverty, humility and service in her relation to Christ. This is by no means to diminish her greatness, but rather to reveal how greatness, when it is of God, lies not in royalty or power as men conceive these things, but on the contrary in the poverty of the humble who are totally dedicated to God's service. Mary's greatness, then, as it is displayed to us in the

Magnificat, is the greatness of her who is blessed and full of grace in the very heart of her poverty as servant of the Lord.

That the conciliatory text on the Virgin Mary became the sixth chapter of the dogmatic Constitution on the Church emphasizes the fact that the Church is the poor servant, for Mary herself is the first of Christians and the type of the Church.

This fresh consciousness of service and poverty in the Catholic Church makes her ready in quite a new way for the ecumenical dialogue. This is being demonstrated in practice: non-Catholics need fear no longer that they will find themselves face to face with the power of the Catholic Church seeking to overcome adversaries, they will rather rediscover brotherly trust in efforts of mutual service and a genuine disposition of poverty and humility. In order to recover visible unity, Christians must understand that they do not possess the truth but are possessed by it. If they wish for mutual enlightenment, it can only be achieved in the spirit of service and poverty appertaining to all those whose gifts have been received in order that they might be given out to all.

The Church asks for forgiveness and extends it

Belief in the holiness of the Church has in the course of history supported an attitude of self-righteousness towards those who are held to be responsible in other Churches. This is not to say that it is because the Church is holy in her faith and sacraments, in that she is an organism of salvation, that she has found it hard to recognize the wounds of sin in her members and hierarchy. But how often might an attitude of humility and repentance have prevented divisions and reconciled those who were separated. We must all regain the strength which comes from the recognition of wrongs committed, from sincere repentance and from mutual generosity, if we are to find again lost Christian unity.

How strikingly did the humility of Pope John XXIII open doors which, it might have been thought, would remain closed for a long time yet. And when in opening the second session of the Council on 29 September 1963, Pope Paul VI uttered words of repentance concerning the divisions, and publicly asked forgiveness for any wrongs done to non-Catholics (which he expressed again at the audience for the Council observers), one was conscious that a new stage had begun in the ecumenical dialogue. More than ever, the Church today needs members of the hierarchy who are truly humble and who recognize wrongs and mistakes, who should ask forgiveness and themselves extend it to all. The holiness of the Church, as the Body of Christ, could not be more truly manifested.

The Church sees a reality in Churches outside herself

An identification of the Roman Catholic Church with the fullness of the Body of Christ and indeed with the Kingdom of God is a rejection of all the baptized who do not explicitly belong to that Church. The Council has been conscious that outside the Roman Catholic Church there is an ecclesiastical reality—not simply of individual Christians who will be saved through their invincible ignorance and good faith, but genuine ecclesial communities (Churches, even, when it relates to the Orthodox) who, although separated from the Holy See, can be instruments of salvation through the faith which they profess, the baptism which they administer, their rites of worship, their love of Holy Scripture and their practice of charity.

The schema on ecumenism seeks to place the greatest possible emphasis on those elements of the Church which are to be found in the ecclesiastical communities separated from Rome. Prayer in common for unity is most strongly encouraged, and the bishops are to foster the ecumenical movement in their dioceses. This is a new, positive and generous attitude towards baptized non-Catholics and the communities to which they belong.

If in other times the Roman Catholic Church has seemed to take up a rigid attitude of expectation, that they should come to her rather than that she should walk side by side with them, it is to be recognized today that the spirit of the Council, which is to say the Holy Spirit who quickens the Church, has considerably modified the attitudes and conditions in both directions.

It is no longer a question of some waiting for the return of the others, nor for these others to retrace their steps, to come back to or to re-enter. Such terms are superseded. It is a matter of moving together along the same way towards Christ who is our future unity, he who himself will bring about this unity of Christians. It is true that the Roman Catholic Church considers that the route is marked by those signs which are dogmas of faith; while we consider that the journey must be inspired by the Word of God in the Holy Scriptures. But it is being increasingly held on both sides that truth in its relation to unity cannot be proclaimed without real solicitude that it be heard and understood by all the baptized. Thanks to John XXIII and Paul VI, thanks to the untiring work of Cardinal Bea and his collaborators in the Secretariat for Christian Unity, non-Catholic observers, invited delegates, are present at the Council to follow this journey of conciliation in which the Roman Catholic Church is in process of discovering in herself all the implications of her teaching tradition. Who would have said five years ago that the dogma defined in the First Vatican Council would have been susceptible of receiving new illumination from the sacramentality and collegiality of the episcopate studied in a General Council? The Roman Church is moving, as we are also, towards a greater light, one that will shine forth from the visible unity of all baptized Christians. In the power of this forward movement, under the impulsion of the Holy Spirit, we are freed from all fear: unity will not be the victory of some and the defeat of others, but the mutual recognition that nothing essential will divide us when our dialogue has matured, when we shall have discovered together all the multiple ecumenical implications of that truth which is our incentive.

We are already united in our baptism, and in our faith

concerning the Trinity and Christ. Our way is the same, for it takes its rise from the single source of baptism and the fundamentals of faith expressed in the Creed. Far from being different, our origin is one and the same. At his coronation and again in the audience for observers, Pope Paul VI applied to the unity of Roman Catholics with other Christians words from St Paul's Letter to the Ephesians: "the same Lord, the same faith, the same baptism" (4. 5). Henceforth we can all openly rejoice in this fundamental unity which exists among us. By baptism we are incorporated in the same body, the Body of Christ; by our faith in the Creed as fundamental, in the Trinity and in Christ, we are one in the glorification of Father, Son and Holy Spirit, of the mysteries of the incarnation, the redemption, the resurrection and the ascension, the gift of the Spirit to the Church, looking for Christ's second coming and the manifestation of the Kingdom of God. Our journey towards the visible unity of Christians consists in mutual enlightenment through dialogue, on this firm basis of baptism and the fundamentals of faith, in order to recognize together the implications of dogma and one day to acknowledge the multiple riches of one truth—all in charity.

Christian people may place great hope in prayer for unity, for if the road be still a long one, yet our hearts are open to all the illuminations it is the will of the Holy Spirit to impart to us.

The Programme of Reform

In the first place the Church came before the Lord in order to ponder on her prayer, her inner attitude as the Bride before her Master, and on her manner of proclaiming the Gospel. This was the essential task of the first session of the Council, which led, in the second session, to the practically unanimous vote for the splendid Constitution on the Liturgy. Then in the second session the Church reflected upon her nature and her structure in the highly important schema on the Church. The major points of consideration here were the sacramental nature of the episcopate, the collegiality of bishops, and the diversities of ministry—that of bishops, priests and deacons. Finally, in the schema on ecumenism, the Church considered her relationship with all baptized Christians. Now she is ready to address herself to questions of her relations with the world at large through the schemata on the Church and the world (schema 13), religious liberty and the Jews.

The liturgy

It is not possible to express here all the merits of the Constitution on the Liturgy. The application of this programme of reform and the work of the commissions which have followed it will gradually reveal all the implications of this considerable and very relevant work of reshaping.

This shows remarkable courage on the part of the Church which, while maintaining her respect for liturgical tradition, is prepared for a sweeping revision of liturgical texts. All of them will be open to detailed study and closer accommodation to original sources and the needs of modern men.

All the work of the liturgical movement of recent years has borne its fruit in the Constitution's insistence on the Church's communal participation in the liturgical celebration. The liturgy is not a collection of rites carried out by priests alone with the aim of ensuring that sacraments are validly administered and the Gospel preached authoritatively. It is seen as the activity of the people of God before their Lord, in which each member, priest or layman, takes his part in praise and prayer according to his charism and proper function.

After centuries of celebration in a purely liturgical language and one foreign to the majority of Catholics, the Roman Church has accepted the widest possible use of the vernacular in the liturgy. The consequences of this decision may well be immense.

The proclamation of the Word of God in readings of holy

Scripture and homilies is given a place of honour and thus the Bible regains its very important position in the rites of worship. Certain occasions envisaged when communion may be given under two kinds, the bread and the wine, make a breach in the wall which the Council of Trent erected in the face of the claims of the sixteenth-century Reformers. Doctrine is not of course changed; but it may be anticipated that occasions when communion is given under both kinds will increase in the future. Thus, in its eucharistic observances, the Roman Church opens the way to the desires of the Eastern Churches and Protestantism.

Finally, among the many significant points of the liturgical reform, mention must be made of concelebration. The fact that a number of priests who have occasion to come together, at a meeting, pilgrimage, or in the conventual life, can together celebrate one eucharist, emphasizes the communal nature of the priesthood and avoids the multiplication of "private Masses" in the same place.

Everything in this fine liturgical reform portrayed here makes a considerable contribution to ecumenism. Throughout, the Roman Church goes forward to meet non-Catholics, while, through fidelity to her actual dogma, she keeps the way towards visible unity unobscured.

The ministry

The most discussed points in the Constitution on the Church were the sacramentality and collegiality of the episcopate, and the diaconate. A clear vote showed the positive attitude of the majority of the Council, and the final result of the voting in the third session, demonstrated the very general acceptance of these subjects by the Council Fathers.

The concept of the sacramentality of the episcopate defines that ministry as essentially distinct from the priesthood. A bishop is not one priest who is set above others, and who has received an addition of sacramental grace to confirm and ordain, and an addition of power, all as an aid in the organization and harmonization of the parishes in the diocese. His ministry is his own and distinct; he receives it through sacramental, episcopal consecration—a particular charism; he is head and father of the local Church, his diocese; he is successor of the apostles; and his ministry or service is liturgical, doctrinal and governmental.

It is true that this concept will deepen problems in the dialogue with those Protestant Churches which do not hold a sacramental view of the episcopate or do not have the episcopate at all. As long as a bishop appeared, at least, as a priest with larger jurisdiction and powers, it was easier to imagine the establishment of episcopacy in those Churches which do not possess it. But while the sacramentality of the episcopate will present a new difficulty in ecumenical dialogue with Protestantism, it should be very much the contrary with Orthodoxy and Anglicanism.

Even so, it is to be remarked that the episcopate appears in a new light and one more in harmony with the Gospel, and in this way its sacramentality cannot but facilitate ecumenical dialogue. In place of descriptions in terms of powers and prerogatives, the episcopate appears much more as a charism, a gift of the Spirit and a ministry in the service of the people of God. The episcopate is a gift from God in order that it may be used in service. A bishop is given to God's people in a local Church to serve them all, clergy and lay people, for the spiritual good of all.

The idea of episcopal collegiality has a very ecumenical aspect. The First Vatican Council had tended to make the pope appear in a certain isolation. The affirmation that bishops as such are united as a "college" in responsibility for the whole Church does much to remove this impression. The actual means of exercising this collegiality have yet to be outlined; but the affirmation of the meeting of bishops around the bishop of Rome, their head, with the care of all the Churches in view, is in itself a deeply ecumenical action.

Discussions on the diaconate, moreover, have shown this concern over the diversification of the ministry for the common good: bishop, priest and deacon are all three of God, invested with a charism, that each may give his own and distinct service to God's people. At the same time, the diaconate displays the Church's pastoral care. Parts of the world such as Latin America, for example, are very short of priests, and the ordination to the diaconate of married men who have proved themselves as laymen in the Church's service would be a great aid in such things as preaching, spiritual guidance and the administration of certain sacraments—baptism, distribution of Communion, even perhaps marriage. It is for the Church, in harmony with the whole great Christian tradition, to define the elements of this ministry for the benefit of evangelization.

Ecumenism

The schema on ecumenism brings to all the Council debates—each of them already with an ecumenical bearing, as we have seen—a completion which directly leads to one of the ends of the Catholic Church's reappraisal, a preparation for visible unity.

The insistence on the unity of all through baptism must once again be recalled here. All baptized Christians are in some measure the Church. It is the starting sign we already possess of visible unity; the solid and sure basis of our complete future unity. Though divided on important points, we have also a common fundamental faith expressed by the "symbols" of the Apostles' Creed and the Creed of Nicaea, in the doctrinal decisions of the first four General Councils, in the two major sacraments, baptism and the Eucharist (leaving aside for the moment the weighty question of the nature of the latter), and through the impulsion to preach Christ's Gospel as it is contained in holy Scripture. Finally, we are profoundly united through our common prayer that the visible unity of Christians may come according to the will of Christ, by his means and in his time. All these things encourage great hope that now the ecumenical movement cannot but go forward more quickly. The pope's pilgrimage to the Holy Land, and his historic meeting with the Ecumenical Patriarch of Constantinople, presented new signs of this splendid hope.

There are still big problems which the ecumenical dialogue will have to examine in depth. But the signs that it is truly our wish to follow without fear the path towards unity have already appeared.

It has often been said that a declaration by the Roman Catholic Church on religious liberty would be a very important gesture. The text presented at the end of the second session is well fitted to make this step so long awaited by many. It is to be hoped that it will be adopted in the third session, after necessary amendments, but not any that will weaken its character as an event of note in ecumenism.[1]

A grave problem which arises in ecumenical dialogue and which constitutes a kind of test for the future is that of mixed marriages between Catholics and non-Catholics. On the basis of unity in baptism and fundamental faith, may it not be possible to evolve a more liberal canon law, perhaps on the following lines?

It is not sufficient to consider this problem only from the pastoral point of view, stressing dangers and providing guarantees. It must be taken on genuine ecclesiological and sacramental foundations.

(*a*) A marriage of two baptized people, that is to say those who are members of the Body of Christ, even if they are divided by ecclesiastical allegiances, is a valid marriage; the two people are themselves ministers of the sacrament.

(*b*) If the marriage takes place in a Catholic church, then a second blessing should be given by a non-Catholic clergyman, for considerations of ecumenical charity and out of respect for the conscience of the non-Catholic.

(*c*) If, on the other hand, the marriage takes place in a non-Catholic church, the Roman Catholic Church would have the right to require, in return, that a blessing is given by a Catholic priest; the latter would then be the witness

[1] Final voting on it has been postponed until the fourth session (*Editor*).

of the Catholic Church to the marriage and the sign of her recognition thereof.

(*d*) A twofold pastoral effort, carried out harmoniously by both Catholic priest and non-Catholic clergyman, would help the couple to form a spiritual life together and to shape the education of children in the ecumenical spirit, without leading to confusion or religious indifference.

(*e*) With the unity of the family in mind, it is preferable that all the children should be baptized and brought up in that Church which shall be chosen by the couple before the marriage.

(*f*) The choice of the church in which the marriage itself is celebrated needs to be guided in the following way—which of the couple is the most devoted and fully practising, or if there is no clear distinction here, then preferably that of the mother, as she will have the most delicate part in the responsibility for religious education.

(*g*) It is unreasonable for the Catholic Church to recognize the marriage of two non-Christians but not to recognize as valid the marriage of two baptized Christians who are separated by their ecclesiastical allegiance.

(*h*) The present state of affairs in fact militates against the Catholic Church; statistics show that this rigorous attitude leads to mixed marriages in non-Catholic churches. It is to be remembered that, psychologically, two people who love each other are liable to be repelled by a too strict juridical attitude and, on the other hand, attracted by what seems a more generous solution.

(*i*) Pastoral work among those who have incurred excommunication through a mixed marriage in a non-Catholic church presents great difficulties for many priests; often the Catholic tends either to join a non-Catholic Church or to fall into religious indifferentism.

In conclusion, the important task which the ecumenical dialogue must now undertake is a thorough theologial examination of the nature of doctrine, liturgy and the sacraments in the different sections of modern Christianity. In the past, ecumenical discussions have been too dominated by ideas of rights, validity and what is lawful. These are necessary, but they require completion by reflection on the gifts of the Spirit who "breathes where it will" (John 3. 8), on the qualities and fruits of the Spirit which are to be honestly recognized in different Churches, whatever their canonical position.

For Catholic theologians this means a study of the nature of doctrine and the sacraments outside the boundaries of the Roman Catholic Church. What, for example, is the significance of the Eucharist celebrated outside the apostolic succession but with the firm and sincere intention of performing Christ's action in conformity with the primitive tradition of the Church?

Unity will not be achieved by the ecclesiastical and doctrinal victory of some and the defeat of others. In accordance with the words of Pope John, we must walk together. During this journey, we shall learn to know each other better. Through this knowledge we shall realize more and more fully that what unites us is more important and stronger than what divides. A day will come when, being thus pervaded by mutual understanding, we shall see that our divisions are within the same visible Church to which we all belong, and we shall turn to asking God to resolve these internal divisions, without allowing uniformity to impoverish that diversity which is necessary in refound unity.

FR MAX THURIAN

[The above was translated by A. F. Price.]

George H. Tavard

Fr George H. Tavard, born in 1922, is an Augustinian of the Assumption. He was ordained in 1947 and taught theology in England and in the United States. He has written extensively on ecumenical questions (*Two Centuries of Ecumenism* [1960], *Paul Tillich and the Christian Message* [1962], *The Quest for Catholicity* [1963]) and is a consultor of the Secretariat for Christian Unity and a *peritus* at the Council.

THE CALL TO ECUMENISM

My ecumenical vocation corresponded with a progressive personal realization of the meaning of catholicity. Its actual origin seems to have been in a meditation of many years on the works of a French religious writer of the last century, Emmanuel d'Alzon, who founded the Augustinians of the Assumption in 1845. A consideration of his guiding ideas will help us to meet the central issues.

Born into a family which was influenced by the Catholic romanticism of the early nineteenth century, Emmanuel Daudé d'Alzon, as a young seminarian at Rome, was an enthusiastic disciple of the philosophical tradition of the times, especially that of Lamennais from whom he learned a conception of liberty. Writing about the establishment of a new Congregation in a letter in 1844, the young man described the foundations he intended for it as follows:

> The moral basis which I should wish to give to a new Congregation would be: the acceptance of all that is Catholic: openness, liberty. . . . I can think of nothing more conducive to the death of spiritual pride and self-satisfaction than the acceptance of everything good outside ourselves; I can think of nothing which will win over

contemporary people so much as open-mindedness, and I know of nothing stronger in the battle against the present enemies of the Church than freedom.[1]

Thus from the beginning of the life's work of Emmanuel d'Alzon the sense of catholicity was emphasized, the idea of the universality of the Church which is manifested in the moral order by open-mindedness and in the social order by liberty. Catholic liberty is a genuine freedom. Properly understood, its outcome is a spiritual identification with the whole Church. This is not just a formal association with Catholicism, by which one belongs to a Church which is called Catholic, but a real identification which makes one open to the fullness and abundance—the catholicity—of the Church.

For the catholicity of the Church in its complete correspondence to God's design in creation, made known not only by Revelation but also in the human and religious cultures which the Spirit raises up in all peoples, is in fact ecumenicity, recognizing the Church as commensurate with the *orbis terrarum*.[2] The unity of the Church within herself is, therefore, the sign of her ecumenicity: she is the pledge and the means of the future unity of the universe finally established, or re-established, in Christ. Here and now she is the sacramental expression of a mystery whose final manifestation will come with the Last Things: Christ, the essential bond of creation, upholder of the universe, and the keystone of space and time.

A vocation to ecumenism is not, then, simply a call to work for the reunion of Christians. When he was defining the aims of his Congregation in 1877, Emmanuel d'Alzon included: "To strive for the unity of the Church, devoting myself to the ending of schism."[3] He was speaking of an acci-

[1] Siméon Vailhé: *Lettres du P. Emmanuel d'Alzon*, vol. 2, Paris, 1925, p. 185.

[2] On ecumenicity and catholicity, see Tavard: "The Laity and Ecumenism" (*Perspectives*, Chicago, January 1963).

[3] *Ecrits Spirituels d'Emmanuel d'Alzon*, Rome, 1956, p. 303.

dental aspect of ecumenism, what in his time was called "unionism."

Unionism meant working for the reunion of the Churches. This was the great idea which inspired the work of Emmanuel d'Alzon, and the first members of his Congregation, among Eastern Christians. It can be criticized from many angles. Closely connected with the outlook of the Eastern Churches in union with Rome, then called Uniats, this approach involved an attitude of superiority towards Orthodox Christians, looking down on their ancient customs without trying to understand the depth of their theological impulsion. Unionism therefore entailed Latinization, viewing the Eastern rites as temporary phenomena destined in due course to give way to the universal Latin rite. So it confuses unity of rite with unity of faith; and as a rite is the liturgical expression of a theology, it confuses unity of faith with theological uniformity. This, which is really "uniatism", and from which relations between Catholics and Orthodox have suffered for centuries, is a stage in ecumenical relations which has now been superseded.

Moreover, reunion of Churches as it was envisaged by Father d'Alzon concerned only the East; Protestantism was left as a matter of individual conversions. In all this there was a restriction, in that unity was seen in its ecclesiastical aspect, in a dimension of canon law, not as "ecclesial"—as the restoring of all things in the unity of Christ.

Very understandably, too, Emmanuel d'Alzon's conception, affected by nineteenth-century colonialism, does not coincide precisely with the contemporary conception of ecumenism, influenced by the modern theological renewal in particular concerning the nature of the Church, and by twentieth-century awareness of cosmic dimensions. It was, then, while I educated myself in the largeness of d'Alzon's Catholic thought, that I was drawn also to gauge its limits.[1]

[1] On the work of the Augustinians of the Assumption for unity and then ecumenism in the past, see a number of essays in *Mélanges Emmanuel d'Alzon*, Saint-Gérard (Belgium), 1952; Tavard: "The Assumptionists

This was very largely due to my theological studies at the Catholic faculty in Lyons. Through the presence there of Abbé Couturier the city of Lyons was already the centre of what has been called spiritual ecumenism, that is to say the endeavour—led principally by Couturier himself—to achieve a unity among Christians in and through prayer. It was not, however, the direct influence of Couturier and his disciples which directed me towards the contemporary form of ecumenism. In fact I never actually met him, and my first contact with his ideas was made through people who understood them little. I thus acquired a certain prejudice which it took a long time to disperse, and because of which I could never simply and completely identify myself with the cause, or indeed with the formulation of the propositions, of "spiritual ecumenism". The decisive thing for me was simply the spirit in which theology was taught at Lyons. The course was strongly imbued with an ecumenical tone, even if it was not always explicit. The deepest influences are often felt almost unconsciously. No one tried to make us into apostles of ecumenism; but all were seeking to educate us in the fullness of Catholic thought. During this time I was living in the same house as a distinguished Byzantine scholar, Fr Salaville, one of Emmanuel d'Alzon's followers who was most alive to and informed on ecumenical matters. A theologian quite different in nature, the late Fr Martin Jugie, also lived in the house, and this enabled me to compare different methods in theological studies and to ponder contrasting views on the questions of the unity of Christians.

In these surroundings and through my own reflections came the conviction that true ecumenism must now direct itself towards Protestantism. It was essential to turn in that direction if the wholeness of ecumenism were to be achieved. Organizations and communities which had formerly applied

---

and the Work for Christian Unity" (*Eastern Churches Quarterly*, winter 1950, pp. 482–94); *Petite Histoire du Mouvement Oecuménique*, Paris, 1960, pp. 145–9.

themselves to problems of Orthodoxy had found difficulty in understanding because they had not considered the question of ecumenism as a whole. Basically, unionism had meant a winning back and Latinization. But with Protestantism, unionism could have no such meaning because the problem was not that of the reunion of Churches with an ancient ecclesiastical constitution. Ecumenism would then become more difficult but perhaps also more purified, removed further from the long rivalries and jealousies of differing rites, and also less confused by the existence of hybrid Churches as it were, Eastern in their ancient liturgical practices but Latin in attitude and orientation. In order to arrive at the conception of ecumenism as the cosmic dimension of catholicity it would be necessary to study and listen to Protestantism.

From the Orthodox as from the Protestant viewpoint, besides, the problem is not one of doing away with schism or heresy, of the absorption of separated Churches and their reintegration by degrees into Catholic unity. Rather, it is that of learning to think together and the gradual working out of a common theology. Abbé Couturier saw justly when he desired to develop ecumenism as prayer, not in the sense of joining different forms of service, or intercommunion, but of one prayer from all Christians, crowned by the will for that unity which is in the mind Christ. But this is not enough. It is necessary to learn to live together not only in the sphere of prayer but in the sphere of thought. Ecumenism is precisely that common endeavour through which the ecumenicity of the Church displays itself. For this, we must be always ready to adjust our conception of the relations between separated Christians. From polemics we must progress to courteous statement, from that to dialogue; from superficial dialogue, which illumines different approaches to problems and seeks knowledge of the history and thought of "the others", we must go on to profound dialogue which leads into the very heart of the mystery of faith.

A three years' stay in England, and nine years in the

United States in daily contact with the highly diversified Protestantism of America, made this increasingly clear. Ecumenism could not be confined to the reading-desk. Whatever the value of ecumenical study, of solitary meditation on the mystery of unity and the tragedy of separated Christians, nothing could take the place of actual contact with the human minds of Orthodox and Protestants. Catholics who embrace ecumenism cannot confine themselves to a knowledge of Orthodox or Protestant history and theology derived from books. With this kind of information must be combined the understanding gained from direct experience. This leads to a great widening of sympathies, revealing as it does the ways of thought and feeling, the deep responses, of those who do not share all our beliefs.

Ecumenism cannot be an isolated movement in the life and contemporary renewal in the Church. I became more and more convinced that ecumenism cannot grow in the void—it is not one aspect of Catholicism to be placed side by side with other parallel aspects. On the contrary, the ecumenical movement as it has formed itself in the Catholic Chuch overlaps all the blossomings which are making new the face of the Church. If it was necessary, which is hardly the case, to choose which is the most important among them, the liturgical movement might well be given first place. This movement does not rest on its aim to help the faithful to participate more truly in the *opus Dei*, the Church's work of praise. It points to a theology which transcends the teachings of the Schools, which is not scholastic in the narrow sense of the word; a theology which is fully Catholic in its scope, pastoral, raising the spirit while guiding thought, embracing all aspects of the life of Christians in order to transform the life of mankind; a theology of service which responds to all things human in its concern to unfold every dimension of the Incarnation, rather than simply to intellectual traditions which are venerable but not always fundamental. Here, the return to the Fathers of the Church, so characteristic a mark of contemporary theology, was brilliantly anticipated by Emmanuel d'Alzon. "The study of the Fathers", he wrote, "has become indispensable to Catholics today."[1] With this, he anticipated the liturgical renewal in its ecumenical dimension; he wrote in 1864: "Unity will have returned when we can say *Unum corpus, multi sumus omnes qui de uno pane participamus*. The more we partake of the Body of Jesus Christ the further will unity shape itself. We must foster love of our Lord Jesus Christ in the Eucharist."[2]

If I owe my ecumenical vocation to the study of d'Alzon's thought, which indeed meant a great deal to me, it must also be repeated that certain weaknesses spring to the eye. His thought is marred by "uniatism", the inaccurate setting out of the problems of Eastern Christianity, treating it as a matter of almost exotic customs and rites rather than the consistent spiritual development from the thought of the Greek Fathers of the Church. Nor are Anglicanism and Protestantism taken seriously enough. D'Alzon's writings on the Oxford Movement are inadequate, although he knew its history well. He misunderstood its significance, seeing it as essentially a move towards Rome, and interpreting the Anglo-Catholicism which survived the conversion of Newman as the triumph of the "Protestant principle of individualism". He understood little of the religious depth of Lutheran and Calvinist Protestantism, seeing in them above all the law of "variations" recognized and described by Bossuet, one of his intellectual masters. In all this, Father d'Alzon was a man of his time, the time of Jaime Balmès and his work on *Protestantism compared with Catholicism* and of ultramontanism of which Father d'Alzon was an enthusiastic advocate at the First Vatican Council. In paying homage to his memory and his undoubted genius, there is no obligation to follow the limited or dated aspects of his thought.

What is the future for ecumenism? Essentially, it lies in the manifestation of the ecumenicity of the Church, which is

[1] Quoted in Athanase Sage: *Un Maître Spirituel du Dix-Neuvième Siècle*, Rome, 1958, p. 12.
[2] *Op. cit.*, p. 103.

what I have called the cosmic quality of her catholicity. Urgent though they are, the relations, friendly or unfriendly, between separated Christians are only a stage, taking up a long moment, in the development of this ecumenicity. At the same time, the immediate problem of Christian reunion is accompanied by that, no less vital, of relations between Christians and Jews; and thirdly there is the vast question of the relations with the great non-Christian religions. This demands, or will demand, a new study of and meditation on what is religion itself and its numberless expressions, which must in turn bring further consideration of the Church's mission in the world and those aims and endeavours which are usually called the missions.

Concern for ecumenism is in fact, then, concern for the whole renewal of the Church. It is St Paul's "anxious care for all the churches"; John XXIII's pastoral concern when he called the Church to Council to renew it inwardly in order to present to the world the spotless face of its divine origins. At its heart is the longing to re-establish the genuine "prophetic office" in the Church, the freedom of God's children to hearken to the Spirit who protects the Church while guiding her among the storms and rocks of every age, the call of Bride to Bridegroom which concludes the Apocalypse and on which the Church sustains her patience in the long wait for his Coming. That climax, no more imaginable in the form it will take than in its date, will be the anticipation in history of the eschatological unity of the Church, a change of condition in which the often mistaken, transient forms of the journey will give place to the glorious recognition of Christ Pantokrator, the divine heart of the universe.

[This contribution was translated by Rachel Attwater.]

Gustave Thils

Gustave Thils is a professor of theology at the University of Louvain and a member of the Secretariat for Christian Unity.

ECUMENISM

Ecumenism is a fashionable word. Like Edmund Rostand's celebrated tirade on Cyrano de Bergerac's nose, it is spoken in many different tones: with enthusiasm, with conviction, ironically, sceptically. In this essay I should like to explain what the word means at present, ignoring everything to do with the history of the word *oecumene*, and the history of attempts in past ages to reunite separated Christians. My plan will be rather of a pastoral nature. The word "ecumenism", in fact, does not directly mean a doctrine, but rather a movement, and it is therefore the theory or theology of this movement that I now mean to develop, proceeding point by point, in a somewhat systematic and even scholastic manner, for the sake of clarity.

I. *The unity of the Church and the disunity of Christians*

1. Christ the Good Shepherd wills that all who are his should be united in one single flock: one alone, in fact, is the people of God, one alone is the Spouse of the Lord, one alone the Temple set on the mount, to which all nations will go up, one alone the Church, instituted by Jesus Christ and ever filled with life by the presence of the Holy Spirit.

The People of God, then, possesses *uniqueness*, but also *unity*. First of all *invisible* unity, that which comes from the Spirit of God, received by faith, in baptism, which two things make us one single body, living and dwelling in charity. *Visible* unity also, in its constitution and structure, displayed in the profession of the Gospel, in the exercise of sacramental worship, and in submission to the lawful pastors, the bishops united under the direction of the successors of Peter.

It is well to emphasize this double aspect of the Church's unity. That unity is clearly shown in the inspired Scriptures, which stress the role of the Spirit, in whom the faithful are one body, and who distributes his many different gifts and graces. They often recall, too, the unifying role of the κοινωνία in Christ and the life in faith and charity, and they stipulate that the Church has her leaders and pastors, who are "the ministers of the mysteries of God" and the guarantee of the unity of the Christian people.

The presence and union of these two elements, Leo XIII wrote, is absolutely necessary to the true Church, somewhat as the intimate union of soul and body is necessary to human nature. The Church is not a sort of corpse; it is the body of Christ, living by his supernatural life. The mystical body is the true Church by the fact that its visible constituents derive their strength and life from the supernatural gifts and the other virtues, whence flows their peculiar nature and meaning: *unde propria ipsarum ratio ac natura efflorescit.*[1]

I purposely stress these two necessary aspects of the Church's unity. When we speak of the "members" of the Church, we are thinking specially of the visible aspect of that unity, and we define the "member of the Church" by all the elements of that visible unity; profession of faith, worship, submission, etc. This clearly appears in our common distinction between "living members" (in a state of grace) and "dead members" (in a state of mortal sin). Christ has told us, in fact, that there will be both just men and sinners in the Church during her earthly pilgrimage. But the separated Christians place the accent very much on the elements of supernatural, invisible unity. Since we acknowledge—and many theologians have written so—that they are practically all sincere, *bona fide*, they can, like us, be either just men or sinners: they can, therefore, live in the

[1] *Satis cognitum*, of 29 June 1896; *Acta Sanctae Sedis*, 28 (1895–6), p. 710.

invisible unity of the Church, by faith and baptism in the Spirit, and by the κοινωνία in charity. Now that is the factor which decides who will be members of the heavenly Jerusalem, whereas the "dead members" of the Catholic Church will be in hell. Consequently, the fact that we are "completely" members of the Catholic Church must not give us a superiority complex which is out of place and in many respects unfounded, and the fact that we do not recognize a separated Christian as a "member" must not make us think that he has no bond with the Church in her supernatural unity.

2. But to proceed: Christians are in fact "disunited", Christian communities are disunited. In speaking of "disunion", I simply wish to express a *fact*, not to make any theological judgement, for it is certain that the blame is not all on one side. The great Councils of Florence and the Lateran and Trent proclaimed, sometimes vehemently, that the Church must be renewed and restored, *in capite et in membris*. Was not that an admission that there were abuses and errors? It is to Hadrian VI of Utrecht, a former professor of Louvain, that we owe the most daring papal declaration on the faults of the Church. In the consistory which he held on 1 September 1522, he attacked the Roman Curia, before the astonished, displeased and sometimes scandalized cardinals. In the instructions which he gave to his Nuncio, Francis Chieragati, for the Diet of Nüremberg, he said in substance: "We frankly own that God has permitted this persecution of his Church because of the sins of men, and especially of the priests and prelates. . . . Well we know that for many years past, *in hac sancta sede*, abominable crimes have been committed. . . . We ought all, then, to humble ourselves, examine ourselves, correct ourselves, and first of all in the Roman Curia, so that correction may begin where corruption started."[1] On the other hand, it would be surprising if, on the side of the Reformers and their disciples,

[1] C. Mirbt, *Quellen zur Geschichte des Papsttums*, 5th ed., Tübingen, J. C. B. Mohr, 1934, p. 261.

there were no faults, no errors, no excesses. Admittedly, the literary style of Catholic historical writing about Photius, Huss, Luther and Calvin has been transformed, but not so far as to exclude the essence of the complaints, notably in the field of the doctrine of the notion of Christianity.

In our day more and more Christians, both Catholics and others, are coming to realize the scandal of the very fact of disunion. It is inexpressibly painful to be faced with a multiplicity of Christian communities, disunited, but praying in common, with moving sincerity, their one Lord's prayer: *Ut unum sint.* It is paradoxical to defend Christianity by quoting: "By this all men will know that you are my disciples, if you have love for one another", when we have at once to admit that these disciples are disagreed, sometimes profoundly. It is humiliating to admit that Christianity, "the religion of love", is presented to non-Christians by witnesses who are divided—Catholic, Methodist or Anglican missions—and sometimes opposed. It is a triple scandal, which can leave no Christian unmoved or indifferent.

But it is not only human proposals that are in evidence; it is divine Providence, it is the Holy Spirit who today calls on Christians to work for union. These are the words of the Instruction of the Holy Office, *Ecclesia Catholica*, of 20 December 1949: "In many parts of the world, whether because of outward events and the change of inward dispositions or, above all, through the united prayers of the faithful under the inspiration of the grace of the Holy Spirit, the hearts of many among those who are separated from the Catholic Church have been filled with an ever-growing desire that all those who believe in Christ our Lord should be one."[1] Fr Boyer, Director-General of *Unitas*, in a lecture given at Rome in December 1948, declared to his Catholic listeners: "It is greatly to be desired that they should be aware of the concern which is moving the non-Catholics, and that they should co-operate with all their might in the

[1] On the whole subject of the Instruction *Ecclesia Catholica*, cf. *Acta Apostolicae Sedis*, 42 (1950), pp. 142–7.

work of Providence." He went on: "How can we help seeing an invitation of Providence in this yearning for lost unity, which from the beginning of the century has been troubling so many of our separated brethren? Whether we wish it or not, something is now changed."

II. *Conversion and Ecumenism*

Among those who work for the union of Christians, clearly distinct tendencies can be discerned, and when we say "tendencies" we are thinking of distinct aims, distinct activities, etc. What are they? There is, first, the work of "conversion" to the Church, which should rather be called "coming" to the Church: next, there is the work of "ecumenism".

1. What do we mean by the "work of conversion"?

There is a "coming to the Catholic Church" or "conversion" when, (1) a Christian—or a group of Christians—comes over to the Catholic Church, (2) because he, or it, finds in this coming over the solution of a personal religious problem, that is, one concerning the way of eternal salvation, (3) without intending, directly or expressly, to exert any influence either on the community he comes from or on the Catholic Church which he enters, and into which he is incorporated (although obviously he does exert, necessarily, a certain influence). Here, briefly expressed, we recognize the process of conversion which is seen, for example, in a missionary region. Such an activity is good. Christ himself sent out his apostles, saying: "Go, make disciples—μαθητεύσατε—of all the nations, baptizing them in the Name of the Father and of the Son and of the Holy Ghost, teaching them to observe all my commandments."

A word in addition: why look for any other word in place of "conversion"? Simply for the sake of accuracy. Every "coming" to the Catholic Church implies, of course, a step which under certain aspects can be called "conversion". But, on the other hand, when we consider the whole process of incorporation into the Church and the personal feelings of those who are incorporated, the word "conversion" is sometimes so unsuitable that we may wonder whether, for the sake of truth and equity, it should not often be forbidden.

2. What, then, do we mean by "ecumenism" or "ecumenical activity"?

"Ecumenism" exists when (1) a Catholic and another Christian—or, again, a group of Catholics and a group of separated Christians— "encounter" each other and engage in a "dialogue", (2) in so far as they are in some way "representatives" of their respective communities (whether by their "Catholic" or "Lutheran" way of life, or by their theological knowledge, or in virtue of a delegation granted by their ecclesiastical authorities), and this (3) in order to know and esteem each other better, to co-exist more pleasantly, to collaborate when circumstances allow, to reflect together on the condition of what they have in common, and above all to work to make the very physiognomy of their respective communities more pure and beautiful, (4) in such a way that the union of the disunited Christians may thereby be promoted.

It is now time to underline certain elements of the brief description I have given.

It is a matter of "encounter" or "dialogue". The question of the lawfulness of these encounters has been settled long ago, since the Instruction *Ecclesia Catholica* of the Holy Office, dated 20 December 1949, permits these encounters, lays down certain conditions for them and even recommends them when they are properly prepared. The problem is therefore one of manner, not of principle.

The two participants meet above all as representatives of their communities. They are not primarily concerned with a personal religious problem but, in and through each other, "Catholic" and "Lutheran", they are interested in "Catholicism" and "Lutheranism". In this encounter the Catholic deals with "Lutheranism" through the "Lutheran", and the Lutheran deals with "Catholicism" through the "Catholic". The term "representative" can here be justified in all the senses it bears in common use: living image of a community, perfect knowledge of a community, authentic delegation by a community.

By this confrontation, as in all ecumenical activity, their direct and explicit intention is to know each other better, to judge each other more fairly, to collaborate and pray together when that is possible, to reflect together on the problems common to the communities to which they belong, and in any case to act in every way so that the visible aspect and physiognomy of their communities may be more perfect, more faithful to the wishes of Christ and his Gospel.

All these benefits are the *finis proximus* of ecumenism: they are real benefits, which are their own sufficient justification: *Idem actus numero . . . non ordinatur nisi ad unum finem proximum, a quo habet speciem.*[1] If I were asked to define a still more general purpose of these ecumenical activities, I should answer that through them, in the long run, fraternal charity is better practised, fairness and truth are more respected, Christianity is purified, the unity of the Church is better prepared, Christ is more glorified in his work, etc. These are the remoter ends, among which, as we have seen, there is included the mutual approach, the union of Christians, in fact, the unity of the Church. But we must avoid schematizing the theology of ecumenism in that really too facile manner which makes "encounters" the immediate end and "incorporation" the ultimate end. Ecumenism aims at the "encounter" of the two parties, in the widest sense of the word, with all the benefits this brings, but no more. It is clearly certain that in this way it renders a service, in actual fact and in many ways, to the Church and her unity. The recent history of the relations between the Pope, Patriarch Athenagoras and Dr Fisher are a striking example of this.

III. *The ecumenical "encounter"*

This can take place in many fields, and especially in social and humanitarian work, in prayer and in doctrinal discussions.

[1] *Summa Theol.*, Ia IIae, qu. 1, art. 3, ad 3.

1. "By this all men will know that you are my disciples, if you have love for one another" (John 13. 35). Take, for example, the *social* and *humanitarian* field. I use the term in its widest sense: the problem of world hunger, illiteracy, diseases and natural disasters, birth-rate and housing, wages and the distribution of wealth, etc. In an age when we read every day in the papers how men of the most opposed groups —East and West—can still agree to sit down together in commissions or congresses, in order to secure to some extent the peace of the world, the rights of man and the well-being of mankind, more and more Christians find it intolerable and scandalous when they see that the disciples of Christ are not able, as Christians—and without forgetting or minimizing their differences—to meet together, to plan together, to join and help one another, in the social and humanitarian problems of our day, some of which I have mentioned above.

On the other hand, whenever Christians have combined in these fields, and without any religious indifferentism, to help one another and others (for example, in Germany, for the refugees, and after the earthquakes in Chile), the result has been a genuine benefit, both within the Christian communities who have made the effort and in connection with the evangelization of the non-Christians. This last statement deserves serious consideration. In fact, in proportion as it is true that mutual aid between Christians constitutes a good, all attitudes of separation, narrowness or life apart in this social and humanitarian sector are implicitly condemned. The Christian responsibility of those who refuse to recognize this is very grave.

But in Great Britain and Germany, in fact, initiatives of this sort are numerous, far more than is commonly supposed: it is therefore rather a matter of accentuating a movement already widely in existence.

2. As for *prayer in common*, in an age when anti-religious propaganda is being organized with uncommon skill and spite, all men of goodwill are glad to be able to testify that they are united at least by the silence or the prayer they offer

to their God, even if they are not agreed as to how they call upon him. This fact makes it more and more unedifying that "Christians", who have so many religious values in common, find it almost impossible to pray in common, and sometimes seem blind to the reasons which should impel them to give the non-Christian world the example of a fundamental unity in adoration, thanksgiving, petition and reparation. Many Christians are hoping—subject to the reservations I am about to mention—not only that certain exceptions may be tolerated but that forms of prayer may be encouraged which might help Christians, or certain circles among them, sometimes to achieve unanimity in prayer.

These initiatives, of course, are not exempt from difficulties and obstacles: they are misinterpreted by some, owing to their training, or to the history of religious differences in their part of the world; they are exaggerated by others, in virtue of a certain doctrinal indifferentism. Action in this domain must only be undertaken with full knowledge and intent. It must still be considered an ideal to be able (while regretting existing divergences) to find a certain unanimity in silence and prayer. We must still promote and encourage the lesser forms of religious unanimity, which can benefit some particular region. And we must still educate the faithful in the true "ecumenical" and "universalist" meaning of prayer in common, so that the desires of the *potior pars* of the faithful may not always be sacrificed to the other Christians, who are certainly more numerous, but are still at a lower level of ecumenical and missionary awareness.

The Holy Office's Instruction *Ecclesia Catholica* itself permits and provides for the common recitation, in ecumenical gatherings, of the Lord's Prayer or a prayer approved by the Catholic Church, and therefore of a prayer from our biblical, patristic or liturgical treasure: the choice is consequently very wide.

3. Finally, *doctrinal discussions*. "Where two or three are gathered in my name, there am I in the midst of them" (Matt. 18. 20). Catholic theology has generally applied this

test to doctrinal gatherings as well as to gatherings for prayer. Our present age is already accustomed to the idea of intellectual solidarity (in scientific research, etc.) and technical also; so much so that the absence of "encounters" or "meetings" between those who genuinely represent the spiritual view—theism, Christianity—*ipso facto* gives them a reputation, not for firmness and stability, but for self-sufficiency, sectarianism and even, among intelligent men of action, for incapacity to promote their ideas. And many are surprised to observe such a lack on the part of Christians, who yet claim to be responsible for the message of the Gospel and even to be defenders of the natural law. They would naturally have expected Christians to take the lead in gatherings devoted to maintaining and promoting belief in the spiritual, in theism and Christianity.

Many Christians would welcome such initiatives, seeing in them a proof of good qualities: vitality, breadth, a sense of realities, competent zeal, universalism and unselfishness. To be frank, it is the absence of such initiatives which is a problem to many: they wonder how, in our age of doctrinal chaos on essential values, such an omission can be justified in the minds of those who have received the mission and the command to be witnesses to the truth, what valid reasons can be adduced for such a result. No doubt, they do not see certain difficulties in every common undertaking; but do the others see clearly enough the considerable benefit being denied to men, societies and Christianity, by abstention and refusal?

These gatherings are only profitable if they are confined to professional theologians and well-prepared laymen, for the real problems are complex and delicate, such as membership of the Church, validity of ordinations, the exact meaning of papal prerogatives, tolerance and the freedom of faith, etc. What is most harmful to this sort of gathering is the presence of amateur theologians, on the look-out for originalities, and amateur laymen, eager for novelties with which to stimulate conversation at their next cocktail party!

IV. *The condition for ecumenical work*

One condition of capital importance in ecumenical work is to recognize, in principle and in practice, the Christian patrimony present among our separated brethren. What is this patrimony? What does this "recognition" imply?

1. On the importance of the Christian patrimony present in the Christian communities separated from Rome, countless testimonies could be quoted: the testimony of deeply spiritual men like Lord Halifax or Abbé Couturier, great initiators like Dom Beauduin, great bishops like Cardinal Mercier, great popes like Leo XIII, saints like Clement Hofbauer. We could quote them endlessly, but I shall confine myself to recalling some papal documents, because of their authority, and the quality of wise prudence which it is such a joy to recognize in them.

The popes have repeatedly alluded to the Christian "patrimony" possessed by the Christian communities separated from the Catholic communion, particularly, need we say, by the Eastern Churches. Many theologians have emphasized the fact that the official ecclesiastical documents use the term "churches" to denote them: "those Churches of the East, so illustrious by the faith of their fathers and their ancient glory".[1] In the apostolic Letter I have just quoted, Leo XIII even said that the differences which divide the Easterns from us are not so great: "moreover, apart from some points, we are in agreement on the rest, so much so that for the defence of Catholicism we even borrow evidences and arguments from the doctrines, the customs and the rites of the Easterns".[2] The fact is, as Pius XI explained, that they have preserved a considerable part of the divine Revelation; they offer a sincere worship to our Lord, they display a special love and devotion to his immaculate

[1] See the numerous references in Y. Congar, *Chrétiens Désunis*, 1937, (Engl. trans. *Divided Christendom*), pp. 381–2, with additions in *Irénikon*, 1950, pp. 22–4.

[2] Apostolic Letter *Praeclara gratulationis*, 20 June 1896, *Acta Sanctae Sedis*, 26 (1893–4), p. 707.

Mother, they have the use of the sacraments".[1] In short, the "gold-bearing particles", to quote Pius XI's expression,[2] are many and precious. As for Pius XII, he expressly required the faithful to appreciate and esteem the Christian patrimony living in the heart of the separated Christians of the East. "All the esteem which is their due must be given to all the elements which, as a patrimony, have been bebequeathed by the ancients to the nations of the East, as regards the sacred liturgy, the priestly Orders, and also other elements of the Christian life, provided they are in perfect agreement with the true faith and the standards of good morals."[3]

But we are not concerned only with the East. Without losing sight of the real differences which divide Catholics from Anglicans, Lutherans and Calvinists, the popes do not forget their state as Christians. They "acknowledge Jesus Christ as Son of God and Saviour of the human race".[4] They are for the most part validly baptized and therefore endowed with the supernatural fruits of baptism. "As many of you as were baptized into Christ have put on Christ" (Gal. 3. 27); "By one Spirit we were all baptized into one body" (1 Cor. 12. 13). They also accept the precepts of Christian morality and the sovereignty of Christ over society and the world. But surely all this is already the effect of divine grace? Yes: here we have "gifts which are in them by the grace of God".[5] Those gifts are a definitive value, which they can never deny.

Declarations of this kind are not isolated, but there can be no question of making a complete list of them.[6] Others can be found, moreover, which, if not opposed, are at least dif-

[1] Encyclical *Rerum Orientalium*, 8 Sept. 1928; *Acta Apost. Sedis*, 20 (1928), p. 287.

[2] See *Osservatore Romano*, 10–11 Jan. 1927.

[3] Encyclical *Orientalis Ecclesiae*, 9 April 1944; *Acta Apost. Sedis*, 36 (1944), p. 137.

[4] Leo XIII, Encyclical *Satis cognitum*, *Acta Sanctae Sedis*, 28 (1895–6), p. 738.

[5] Instruction *Ecclesia Catholica*, *Acta Apost. Sedis*, 42 (1950), p. 144.

[6] Cf. G. Baum, *L'unité chrétienne d'après la doctrine des Papes, de Léon XIII à Pie XII*, Paris, Ed. Cerf, pp. 66–85.

ferent in tone and perspective. From all that precedes I shall therefore conclude only this, that in the mind of the hierarchy there is a real doctrinal current which emphasizes the importance of the Christian heritage present in the separated Christian communities, and reminds Catholics of the esteem which should be given them. This current is growing in breadth, especially in ecumenical circles. May I add that this current seems to me, objectively speaking, an advance? I grant of course that those Catholics to whom the separated Christians are purely and simply "non-Catholics" certainly have a point. A Calvinist is certainly not a Catholic! But this "negative view", as it has been called, does not and cannot do justice to all the Christian reality of two believers who are compared together. Only a "positive vision" can claim to do that: one which at least looks at the two parties in the light of their respective achievement as Christians.

2. But these values must be acknowledged *concretely* and really.

If we neglect to take account, concretely and really, of the Christian patrimony of the separated brethren, if we define them solely in terms of what they are not, or not entirely, can we say that our judgement is realistic and fair? And this very "negative" attitude will find expression in a theology, a juridical status, a prayer, etc., of an equally negative spirit. On the contrary, really taking account, in both ideas and actions, of the Christian patrimony of our separated brethren will mean a fundamental change of attitude; we shall consider one another as "brothers", up to a certain point, sometimes very advanced; the theological position of the other party will be thought out in function of that partial but sometimes considerable common area of gifts; an ecclesiastical discipline will be established which does justice to the actual condition of those for whom we legislate; it will be considered self-evident that sometimes, in determined circumstances, a unanimous prayer may lawfully be used in common. In short, the "lighting" will be different, and so will the vocabulary used to denote the "others", and the doctrine elaborated to "explain" the others, and the attitude adopted for "encountering" the others, etc.

That is one reason why all ecumenical undertakings are very delicate in themselves, both for one who has to carry out their pastoral application and for one who tries to outline their theological justification. But this is the price which must be paid for a greater loyalty to the principle of "recognizing", both in thought and in action, the real Christian condition of our separated brethren.

This work is a gradual course and progresses slowly. But it can no longer be said that Catholic theologians regard the separated communities only as "synagogues of Satan", nor that Protestant theologians see Rome only as the "modern Babylon".

V. *The main purpose of ecumenism*

1. We have seen that the ecumenical "encounter" takes place between two spokesmen, "representative" of their respective communities, in order to produce a better coexistence, by "ameliorating" the physiognomy and the actual condition of those communities. Now in ecumenism, as in everything else, one must first set one's own house in order. The Lutheran will work to make his community more faithful to the will of Christ; the Catholic will do the same; and thus, in this simultaneous effort of total fidelity to the Gospel, a certain *rapprochement* will in fact be achieved.

That was certainly one, if not the chief, intention of John XXIII when he summoned the Council. He said, and often repeated, that he desired to bring about in the Church a restatement, an *aggiornamento*, a spiritual "renovation", a "renewal" of strength, so that she might appear in all her beauty. Thus, for example, in his address to the diocesan directors of Italian Catholic Action, in the beginning of August 1959: "By the grace of God we shall, then, convoke the Council, and we mean to prepare for it by having in view whatever most needs to be strengthened and reinvigorated in the union of the Catholic family, following the plan of our

Lord. Then, when we have accomplished this laborious task, by eliminating all that could be an obstacle on the human plane to a rapid progress, we shall present the Church in all her splendour, *sine macula et sine ruga*."[1]

Evidently the Council, by this intention, is doubly ecumenical (no paradox is intended): first in the sense of a "general" Council but also in the sense of the ecumenical renewal, with which we are now concerned.

2. This renewal, to speak more concretely, implies that the Church must make her ecumenicity more fully actual, precisely with regard to the separated Christians. But what is this "ecumenicity" and what does it imply with regard to the separated Christians?

(*a*) What is meant by "ecumenicity"?

The full catholicity of the Church includes a mystery of unity and a grace of diversity, both equally essential, which are now frequently described (and rightly, but I cannot prove it here) by the name of ecumenicity. We all know those words of Scripture, telling us that to the Church there is neither Jew nor Greek, barbarian nor Scythian, slave nor free, for all are one in Christ (Col. 3. 11), and also that very significant allusion to the task devolving on the "good stewards of God's varied grace":—καλοὶ οἰκονόμοι ποικίλης χάριτος Θεοῦ (1 Peter 4. 10). This can only mean that the expansion over all the world—κατα τῆν οἰκουμένην—of the only Church, one and catholic, implies, first and negatively, the rejection of every form of particularism and uniformity not really required by true and genuine unity: second and positively, the integration and actualization in, and in virtue of, the unity of the Church, of all legitimate differentiation and plurality.

In the use of this term we can observe different emphases. When Catholics speak of ecumenicity in connection with their own Church, they emphasize the aspect of "diversity" and "variety", no doubt because among themselves unity

[1] *Osservatore Romano*, 10–11 August 1959.

seems to be sufficiently guaranteed. But when they look at the ecumenical movement, for example, they insist that ecumenicity is real "unity", no doubt because the multiplicity of member-churches in the World Council of Churches seems to belie the real notion of ecumenicity. When the ecumenical circles of Geneva speak of ecumenicity in connection with the member-churches, they insist on the aspect of communion and unity implied by ecumenicity, but when they turn to the Catholic Church, they insist that ecumenicity implies "variety" and not uniformity, as uniformity seems to them almost a "note" of the Catholic and Roman Church.

That is why Catholic ecumenists tend primarily to give the Church's ecumenicity more fullness, by promoting a "unity" which is not "uniformity", but which demands a legitimate "plurality" and "diversity" in all the elements which constitute the form of Christian life and the type of ecclesiastical existence.

(*b*) What is implied by this ecumenicity of the Catholic Church, from the point of view of the variety and diversity required by her very universality?

Ecumenicity affects the whole life of the Church: Catholics themselves or the "old Churches": the Catholic community confronted with the separated Christians: finally, the Catholic mission or the "young Churches".

First, the "old Churches". That rich and poor, educated people and untaught minds, leaders and subjects, are to be found among Catholics is something plain to view. But we must go further; there are also among Catholics, even in the West, very varying shades and emphases in different regions, in the matter of piety and teaching, Christian life and apostolic activity. An Italian Catholic is not a Dutch Catholic, and a Bavarian Catholic differs from a Rhinelander.

Then, the "young Churches". Recent missionary encyclicals—for example, the *Evangelii Praecones* of Pius XI in June 1959—have never ceased to repeat that the seed of the Gospel and the Church can grow and expand in every nation, whatever the spirit, race, culture, economic system or social condition of the inhabitants—on condition, of course, that these elements can be assimilated into Christ.

Finally, with regard to the separated Christians. From this point of view, ecumenicity signifies in practice, first, that the Church is not bound by any particularism or uniformity in the matter of rite, spirituality, theological system, religious sensibility or ecclesiastical discipline, with the obvious exception of what is postulated by the undoubted demands of her genuine unity; second, that the Church can assume, and must integrate, in her unity itself, the plurality of forms and diversity of emphases in the matter of rite and piety, religious sensibility, theological systems, usages and customs, the form of Christian life and the style of ecclesiastical existence.

Accordingly, when Catholics exalt the importance of the Word of God, when they stress the place of the Bible in Christian spirituality, when they emphasize the transcendence of God and the free gift of grace, when they draw attention to the role of faith in the sacramental life, etc., how should we interpret these things? Does it mean, as is sometimes said, that Protestant traditions are being introduced into Catholicism? No, not necessarily. It may be an attempt to "actualize", more or less, the most authentic ecumenicity of the Church. To "actualize", in the heart of the one and only Church, the marvellous diversity of spiritualities, religious sensibilities, doctrinal preferences, etc., is to accomplish and perfect ecumenicity.

At the same time, it is to make the Church truly the home of all: "habitable" by all, and so loved by all. For it is not enough to say that, in order to be in communion with the Catholic Church, a separated Christian ought not to deny any good thing which by God's grace is present in him and the community to which he belongs.[1] It is also, and above all, necessary that in the Catholic Church the separated Christian should be able to find himself truly at home, in "his house", from the fact that here are found, already actualized, the accents and legitimate forms of Christian life which are

[1] Instruction *Ecclesia Catholica*, as above, note 11.

dear to him in the realm of piety, spirituality, doctrinal witness, style of church life, etc.

The activities of which we have given some examples above are therefore "accomplishing" the Church's ecumenicity. They add a new colour, an original brilliance, to the variegated beauty of the Spouse of Christ. They constitute a happy completion of the "home" of the people of God. They are not things which inevitably cause confusion or weakening: far from it. They can be a part of the providential task for which all the faithful ought to work, willingly and ardently. "Actualizing" the ecumenicity of the Church is, then, one of the main purposes and, no doubt, *the* main purpose of Catholic ecumenism.

Conclusion

What, then, is ecumenism? We can now conclude that ecumenism is: (1) a movement, that is, a totality of intentions and efforts, of prayers and studies, of activities and declarations, of gatherings and institutions, (2) which tries, (*a*) by "encounters" in the widest sense of the term (social, doctrinal devotional) between Catholics and other Christians "representative" of their respective communities, (*b*) to actualize more fully the multiform "ecumenicity" of the Church (in her piety, customs, theology, etc.), (*c*) and thus, in consequence (notably by reason of the changes which result from it in the Church), to facilitate the *rapprochement* and the union of the now disunited Christians.

[This contribution was translated by P. J. Hepburne-Scott.]

Maurice Villain, S.M.

Fr Maurice Villain, S.M., is well known for his life of Abbé Couturier of whom he is an active disciple, and his introduction to ecumenism (*Unity—A History and Some Reflections*, London and New York, 1963).

A SPIRITUAL HERITAGE

Where the sin of all men has entered, breaking and separating, there, if superabundant grace is to enter and repair, a great number of souls in all the Christian groups must be generously open and welcoming to it. Then, like "burning and shining lamps" (John 5. 35), hosts of "Christbearers" will diffuse throughout the Christian body such a spiritual and unifying tension that the "Christophany" of the whole will burst on all men's eyes. The intensity of the Christian life will have brought back unity in faith and preserved the lawful and fruitful diversity of the different families of minds, cultures and races.

PAUL COUTURIER.

The antecedents

A young doctor of divinity, fresh from the moulds of the Roman faculties in the years 1925–30, was of course totally unprepared for any possible ecumenical task: that was not surprising, for that specialist work was not yet included in the ministries of the Church. But also, the integral structure of his theological training and, even more, the mentality that it had impressed on him, might have been thought to make such a task highly improbable.

For what was the theological baggage which he brought back with him? A rigid and literal Thomism, tightly crammed into the "Twenty-four Theses", which the Dominican Fathers of those days held as an article of salvation, to the accompaniment of the old commentators, from Cajetan to Billuart. A man like Sertillanges, who tried to bridge the gap between St Thomas and the philosophers, was regarded as an innovator. Bergson and Leroy, Laberthonnière and Blondel served Fr Garrigou-Lagrange as tragi-comic foils, and woe betide the rash student caught red-handed reading *Le Milieu Divin*, some duplicated copies of which were circulating covertly! Exegesis claimed to be scientific, but in fact it was dominated by scholastic thought, which always prevailed when it came to the conclusions, and nothing in scriptural methods introduced us to a knowledge of the Bible which was familiar, spiritual and soul-satisfying. Those who hungered for the Word of God had to remain hungry. In those days, which now seem so far off, apologetics reigned supreme and ecclesiology was directed mainly to *demonstrating* the true Church of Jesus Christ. Leaving the *Summa*, the young priest next pored over an encyclopedia, learned, accurate and very convenient, called the *Dictionnaire Apologétique*. Its editor and his collaborators meant to be men of their time; eminent men they were, whose kindness and untiring willingness to help I myself often experienced. They had felt obliged, however, in 1920, to found their programme, with great circumspection, on the axioms of yet another dictionary, which they were refounding and continuing, and which went back to 1888. The epilogue to this monument (dated 1930) sums up those axioms in these words: "To put within the reach, and as it were in the hands, of every reader of good will the principal *proofs* of the Catholic Faith with the soundest *answers* to every kind of objection made against it." This cautious covering note allowed the insertion of some nonconforming articles, which were then like gusts of fresh air, but did not ward off subsequent condemnations. With regard to the world of the Reformation and the Eastern Churches, which enters into the scheme of ecumenism, the young doctor was in a closed circuit. How could he not react with horror against the monster presented by Denifle under the name of Luther? How could he have discovered the treasures of the *pietas anglicana* when the Bull *Apostolicae Curae*, that subtle obstacle, destroyed in advance all the credit of Anglicanism? What fair judgement could he have given on the Orthodox Churches, presented by a man like Jugie through Latin categories? In short, all this material—which was treated without qualification as *extra ecclesiam*—served only as *counter-proof*, to bring into sharper relief the original essence of the Catholic Church.

From his childhood's catechism, in fact, to his doctorate, the young priest nurtured in classial Catholicism had been drilled in the same style of combat, to defend the Church against the attacks and hate of her enemies. The direction, the aim, the ideal were always the same, only at different levels of education. He may have known from his youth up that the word "martyr" meant "witness", but no one had ever told him that the Christian had to "bear witness" (this expression, now almost worn out with repetition, had not yet reached current speech). He had been taught to "overcome human respect", to "defend" himself, or, what was better and easier, to "attack"; the strategy of the pugilist.

The Church as *mystery* or *communion* of believers held a very small place, certainly not the central place, in the curriculum. Fr Mersch had not yet lit up the ecclesiological horizon with his fine volumes on the mystical body, and that doctrine, so central in St Paul, slipped into the manuals only by way of *corollarium pietatis*. Some people were afraid of it, and one bishop said: "That is Protestant!" The Church was defined solely as the society of those who profess the same faith—the one Catholic faith—receive the same sacraments from the authentic priesthood, and are subject to the jurisdiction of the Roman pontiff. The Church as communion of the baptized, with all its overtones and appeals, would have seemed a suspect idea. An insurmountable barrier was erected between us, the privileged, and the unfortunate "heretics" and "schismatics" who lived beyond our borders. The barrier could only be lowered if they returned to Mother Church by signing an abjuration. The Catholic Church, "possessor of the truth": that aphorism was apodictically demonstrated in the manuals; men had only to look at her without prejudice and they could not fail to recognize her transcendence and fall on their knees before her.

I must confess it: the writer of these lines received in its entirety the theological training which he has just outlined. And then in 1929, capped as doctor and appointed professor, he was asked to draw up without further preparation, the bases of a course of ecclesiology, adding to it lessons in ecclesiastical history.

As it is a question of testimony, let me declare it bravely and *without bitterness against anyone*: my Roman training had enclosed me in an air-tight sphere, and had taught me all its perfect joints, its secret works and how to take them to pieces, but the sphere was singularly lacking in openings on the world—a sort of blinded sputnik! Now I was torn with anxiety, tormented by scruples, and the further I progressed in my researches, the less satisfaction I found. No doubt the critical rigour of my old teachers at the Sorbonne and the *École des Chartes* (ten years earlier) had their effect in a timely resurgence. Thirty-five years later, I am still sure of it: an appetite for the study of the sources, an intense love of history, had strengthened me against the excesses of a notional or materializing synthesis, which sooner or later would succumb to the pressure of positive methods. What worried me was precisely the spirit in which ecclesiology and ecclesiastical history were prepared for the use of the students, with a determined apologetical bias. Every judgement on "the Other" was designed to start from the Catholic doctrine, considered in its static condition, and what was more, from the Western and Latin outlook.

But how was I to re-read history? With reference to what criterion could I restore the balance, in the absence of an "ecumenical key", with which no one could supply me? I was imprisoned in a world of ideas, untranslatable to the modern man, and although the idea of a real conversation with a Protestant or an Orthodox never crossed my mind,

I had the suspicion that they could not possibly grasp my arguments unless they were *already* enlightened by a very special grace of the Holy Spirit. I rejected, of course, the caricature of Luther in the Catholic historians. Beneath the quotations from the Reformer which I read, I searched for a meaning in that sincere desire of his to reform a Church which, at the close of the Middle Ages, had cut a sorry figure. When he took the Bible with him in his secession, that action involved grave risks. What ruptures followed! All the same, he took with him the Book of the Word of God, with which to feed the people of God, and in consequence—by a contrast perhaps necessary at first but fraught with danger—the Catholic Church, turning in on herself, obscured the Word by keeping it in Latin, with the result that after four centuries my Christian and priestly training had been cruelly starved of it.

From another point of view, how did God regard Christians whom he had allowed to be born in heresy or schism? Famous Protestants like John Wesley, Alexandre Vinet or Frédéric Oberlin, Anglicans of the stamp of Pusey or Halifax, were they not, in their own way, "saints"? Or to take extreme cases, men like Wilfred Monod or Maurice Goguel, whose works, stamped with a destructive liberalism, I read in exasperation—had they not also written passages which were profoundly spiritual and prayerful, imprinted with the love of Jesus Christ our Saviour? How could I reconcile, on the one hand, this undisguised agnosticism with, on the other, those evidences of deeply Christian souls? No doubt these were embarrassing and regrettable cases, but clear vision and charity would surely have indicated a more finely balanced treatment in their respect? Is not inward uprightness the decisive virtue in the eyes of God, and cannot a fervent Protestant be saved, as well as or even better than a mediocre Catholic? However, with these problems scarcely broached, my "axes" always brought me back to the structure of the true Church as the unique and essential element: the condition, *sine qua non*, of faith and salvation. Finally, by my teaching on the "threshold" of theology, I had to provide the introduction to the course of dogmatics, which was taught by another professor. Of this world of dogmatics I possessed a notional synthesis, static in a way I did not then realize to be so inadequate and dangerous. Despite my difficulties, however, I felt it to be my professional duty to map out my route well and to effect the junction (with dogmatics) carefully. Had I not been told by one of my Roman professors, worried at my preference for positive methods and bidding me goodbye: "Remember, what people want from us priests and religious is—our formulas!"

Ecumenism, as I said, had not then won a place of its own. Yet the Malines Conversations, from 1921 to 1925, had appeared as a sort of example before their time, unofficial but helpful in preparing men's hearts, as Cardinal Mercier affirmed. In so far as I had been able to follow their development, they had excited me. How sad it was, then, when *Documentations catholiques* revealed, with proofs in support, that they had been suspended and had failed. What could I conclude? Several visits to London for research in the British Museum had enabled me to observe that the English Catholic clergy were pleased at this failure. What miserable judgements I heard over there, on Portal, Halifax and the great Cardinal Mercier, those valiant protagonists!

I was less well informed about the first enterprise of ecumenism in the proper sense: the conferences at Stockholm, 1925, and Lausanne, 1929, on which the encyclical *Mortalium animos* had imposed a formal prohibition. It must not be forgotten, of course, when today we recall that severe document, that it censured a departure which was dangerous, liberal in character and anti-Catholic. But we must still admit that nothing in this condemnation of "pan-Christianism" gives us any glimpse of the great and fundamental intention of men like Söderblom and Germanos, and we can now see that the document lacked prophetic inspiration. In fact this vast enterprise, once the period of groping was passed, set itself vigorously in order with the formation of the

World Council of Churches, and since the Amsterdam Conference the climate has completely changed. We regret all the more, then, that haughty language towards our Christian brothers, that cutting phrase, for example: "that it is on no account permissible for Catholics to join in such enterprises or contribute to them; if they did so they would be attributing authority to a false Christian religion, totally alien to the unique Church of Christ". But at that time a more liberal expression would have caused astonishment, for the Catholic Church was still carrying on her monologue with herself. And it was within this closed circuit that I worked as a young professor for seven years.

My meeting with the prophet

It was in January 1936 that I came to know Abbé Paul Couturier, at the opening of the Week of Universal Prayer, of which he was the promoter at Lyons. I only had a few minutes' private talk with him, as we waited for the hall to fill, where my friend Jean Guitton was to give an address. A moment of grace, followed by a long visit, which was repeated every week and several times a week, up to 1948. For twelve years at Lyons, for five years at Paris, I was the closest fellow-worker of that pioneer of spiritual ecumenism. When he died on 24 March 1953 I humbly accepted the legacy he bequeathed me: his books, his archives, the unique treasure of a world-wide correspondence, above all, the sacred mission of handing on his message in its integrity, as he had given me to understand and live it.

If I try to reconstruct my first conversations with him, I must admit that they met with some resistance. Through the intuitions of this man, so highly enlightened in the things of God (although he could not express himself in the manner of a professional in the ecclesiastical disciplines), a new vision, exalting and liberating, of theology and history was suddenly revealed to me. But how hard it was for me to adapt to it my intellectual schemes, engraved and carved in me by daily application to my professional task!

Abbé Couturier's article on "The Psychology of the Octave of Prayer" (December 1935), in which all the essentials of his method are found in germ, was the initial theme of my ecumenical meditations. But it still took me several years to assimilate it vitally, so true is it that a conversion of this kind is not merely an adherence at the intellectual level, but requires a transformation and a commitment of the whole self. The early numbers of *Irénikon* and two pamphlets by Dom Lambert Beauduin completed this mental equipment. From 1937, with the series *Unam Sanctam*, and then with the series *Théologie*, a wholly new literature began, in which the precious ore of ecumenical thought clearly shone. I eagerly read *Chrétiens Désunis* (*Divided Christendom*, London 1939), in which Fr Congar drew up the principles of a Catholic ecumenism, and then *Catholicisme* (English trans. *Catholicism*, London, 1950) by Fr de Lubac. This last was the finishing stroke, for it offered an entirely fresh synthesis of theology in patristic values, worked out at first hand. It was a cluster of original and complementary rays, on the mystery of faith, of which Western scholasticism had deprived us. A whole method of ecumenical theology (though this was not directly the author's intention) could have been drawn from it, if I may say so, before its time. All the same, I owe it to the truth of this testimony to say that it was not these books that taught me ecumenism. For a year, two years, I steeped myself in the spirit of Abbé Couturier, and it was he who both fertilized my reading and provided me with the key to those interdenominational conversations, to which I was devoting myself all the time. I always had the impression, however, that my mystical teacher lived on the heights, much higher than my friends the theologians, and that he saw further, while on all levels of the ecumenical horizon this utterly humble and self-effacing man exercised an attraction without equal. Little words or reflections of his, thrown out in the course of a conversation, have later turned out to be prophetic: his judgement, for instance, in 1938, that the Conferences of Stockholm, Lausanne, Oxford and Edinburgh might well be considered by future historians as the first foreshadowings of an immense ecumenical Council such as Christendom had never known, in which union would be sealed. Spoken at a time when all possible ecumenical avenues were officially barred by *Mortalium animos*, the saying might seem presumptuous. But it pointed in the right direction, then totally unforeseeable. Today it rings true, it points far ahead. And what shall I say of his tracts and pamphlets, which I collected in a book in 1962, while the Second Vatican Council was beginning its first session? Many noticed that these texts weave a discreet counterpart round the Council: from twenty-five years earlier, they distil a spirit, the very spirit which was released at the opening of the Council. Nor is this surprising, for they were among the most effective factors of that spiritual maturity which enabled John XXIII to assign ecumenical goals to his gigantic enterprise.

In the dawn of my vocation, my perseverance was encouraged by a particular factor: Abbé Couturier never left me passive or, if I may put it so, unemployed. He had the singular gift of revealing you to yourself, of bringing you from the outset into a positive, or rather creative collaboration. From the very first day, I shared in his programmes and projects. I set myself to answer his questions, which were unceasing. I made it a point of honour that he should be well documented, and he invited me to follow up his work along new trails. Someone once said: "Charity means receiving." The most unrepayable gift made me by this saint and prophet of cosmic dimensions was this, that while my collaboration might naturally have been limited to services, he allowed me to imprint on his sublime work some marks which are my own.

It would need a book to express adequately all that I owe to the Abbé. Perhaps a general judgement will suffice for a simple indication. I had been a priest for nine years when through contact with him I rediscovered my priesthood and perceived for the first time the mystery of the Church, with a perfectly clear view of an immense new task of the Church, which would be that of the theology of the future. From the beginning I had understood, intensely, something that was then not to be found in writing, that ecumenism is an essential dimension of the Church, left unexplored for centuries. If it could be reinstated at all levels, the face of the earth would be renewed.

On my master's emaciated face, in the depth of his blue eyes, I could read how the "great distress" of division possessed him. All Christians, he said, but Catholics especially, carry in their inheritance this "communal sin". Read history without prejudice and you will find the proof there. Between the Protestants and the Catholics of France lies a trench, filled with the blood of the Wars of Religion. By the mere fact of not taking seriously that scandalous situation, we assume a guilty responsibility and betray the Gospel. It follows that our prayer for unity ought to be in the foreground of our spiritual life and at the level of the prayer of Christ (John 17), and more, it should always be marked by penitence and humility. His campaign of penitence, to disavow the massacre of St Bartholomew, to denounce the persecutions in Spain or South America, touched the Protestants and overcame many prejudices. At Geneva in 1941, when I had occasion to speak on these lines, the effect was immediate. A pastor came up to me and seized my hands with great emotion. "I never thought", he said, "that a Catholic priest was allowed to say such things." Certainly, for four centuries such language had been forgotten, and some bishops even rejected it on the ground of the indefectibility of the Church. But we need no longer justify such existential language since Paul VI, at the opening of the second session of the Council, solemnly pronounced the *mea culpa* of the Catholic Church.

In the second place, he taught us to look at "the other" with love. In virtue of his baptism, the one baptism of Christ, my separated brother is first of all my "Christian" brother, and the mystery of grace which unites us is far more important than what divides us. Christ died for him, as he died for me: Christ loves him as he loves me, and perhaps—

why not?—loves him better: Christ saves him as he saves me, by his death and resurrection, except that he lets him follow a path different from mine. At the heart of this mystery of salvation there is this fact, that God the Father looks on every soul with good will, judging him in proportion to the light he has received from his own Church's tradition, and that is what really counts. The Catholic Church is not the only body which claims to be the sole possessor of the truth, and therefore, however unyielding my faith on this point, I shall banish from my mind all feelings of self-sufficiency and domination. I shall approach my Christian brother in all humility and respect, eagerly learning whatever he has to teach me, enriching myself from what he wishes to give me. Taught by these simple and transparent principles—which have nothing to do with indifferentism—the Catholic speedily escapes from the ghetto in which he had been imprisoned by the classical apologetic, and he discovers dialogue. Is not that exactly what John XXIII gave the whole Church to understand when he founded the Secretariat for Unity and invited the observers to the Council? But to profess these principles thirty years ago was to range oneself among the suspects.

Interdenominational dialogue, in its doctrinal and technical aspect, necessarily follows, and it was towards this that my master's spirituality finally converged: that was not understood by those who thought that he was making spiritual ecumenism an end in itself.

There is no need for me to repeat here what I have expounded at length in his biography. But I must insist that all my discoveries concerning the dialogue with my separated brethren were suggested by the attitudes he taught me through his example. "I have tried", I wrote, "to give a dogmatic expression to something which, in the Abbé, was a meeting of souls and thoughts in prayer, a collecting of seeds, a prolonging of lines. I realized that direct contact overthrew prejudices, re-centred positions which had been thrown out of balance by the classic kind of controversy, and clarified the vocabulary, resulting, in short, in a cordial and open understanding, and this result was no mean achievement." This was the basis of a first draft of a "method of ecumenical theology" which was applied both at the Conferences of Châtelard, for the ecumenical training of priests, and at the interdenominational dialogues at Dombes. It was the fruit of an experience: it was modified from year to year, in accordance with the particular programmes discussed.

This ideal was well worth the consecration of a life. It is not my concern to compare vocations and arrange them in order: every vocation which is in its right place, corresponding to the Lord's will, is noble and great. But it is permissible to state that in the scheme of the Church's renewals, ecumenism is a prophetic work which embraces and crowns all the rest. Those who came across it, thirty years ago, in all its freshness (I mean: freed from ulterior motives of proselytism, which had bedevilled earlier attempts), embraced it enthusiastically, gladly renouncing easier careers and the certainty of success. But they very soon found out that their path, which had to be cleared at every step, was strewn with pitfalls, and that the demons of suspicion, denunciation and condemnation lay in ambush at every corner. It went through the solitude of Gethsemane and led to Calvary, often with no hope of a resurrection on the morrow. "If you would serve the Church," the Abbé used to say, "you must be ready to suffer at her hands": words grounded on experience, which all the good workmen of the early days, those great lovers of the Church, found to be true. Silence, patience, immolation, forgiveness of injuries, these words were dear to my master, and he who had been the "origin" and "source", aspired only to disappear. Those who come to the movement today, when the first fruits are being reaped, have no idea what the days of sowing were like. I trust they will not claim for their own credit what belongs only to God: to him alone be all the glory!

My experiences

To complete my testimony according to the prescribed plan, I should now describe my "experiences". As these cover some thirty years they cannot be summarized in a few paragraphs, so I shall confine myself to a chronological scheme. It will be understood, of course, that this is not a history of ecumenism, but a purely personal angle of vision on that history or on the way in which the Lord has granted me to live it.

The first period was before the war. In those years, 1936 to 1939, ecumenical activities radiated from Lyons, centred on the Week of Prayer for Unity, which had a brilliant start. Meetings for prayer and biblical studies abounded: from time to time we welcomed prominent Anglican, Orthodox or Protestant personalities, and this formed a fresh centre of interest. In 1937 was founded the interdenominational group of Dombes, which continues its work still, with unwearying perseverance. Since 1956 it has produced some important results in ecumenical theology. These years were marked with the incomparable grace of the beginnings.

The second period was that of the war. The labourers were few, but enjoyed complete freedom. We adopted a plan of retreats for prayer and study, the benefit of which was a mutual understanding, springing from our spiritual lives, lived side by side and mutually appreciated. There I gained the conviction that only in those conditions can a fruitful dialogue be begun. At Taizé the young pastor Roger Schutz was clearing his hillside, and I had the privilege of being present at the inauguration of that blessed community, and knowing its graces and its difficulties—a miracle which continues year by year, in intense fidelity to the Spirit. At Grandchamp, Mlle Marguerite de Beaumont humbly prayed, and laid the foundations of the sister community.

The World Council of Churches did not yet exist, but its architect, Dr Visser 't Hooft, appeared with his first companions. I had the good fortune to form some lasting friendships in that early group when it worked at the Bureau de

Champel, before settling in the Route de Malagnou, and from that time I was a discreet but very attentive witness of the preparation of an epic.

I should like to note that the *Invisible Monastery*—that family of souls of all denominations whom the Spirit has sealed with a special vocation to prayer for Christian unity—began to take shape in 1942. The idea forced itself on me that there exists throughout the world a legion of souls who are guided in this direction, but do not know one another. They must therefore be discovered, and a link between them must be established. From time to time a leaflet of meditation and spiritual exchange would channel their intercessions for the most relevant intentions of ecumenism, and these would be offered to the Lord by day and night. The title "Invisible Monastery"—without rule or habit—seemed to me an adequate expression of this idea.

The long post-war period (1945–63) would require a minute analysis, on which for lack of space I cannot embark, and I should run a grave risk of falsifying its inner workings by too simplified judgements. The seeds of ecumenism planted during those terrible years should naturally have flowered in the sun of liberation. To a great extent they did so, but many hopes were to remain in abeyance.

Suddenly the horizon widened, since journeys were again possible. There were then scarcely half a dozen of us to plough the soil of France, in order to plant the Week of Unity, which was spreading an ever closer network by means of the tracts printed at Lyons. But the vital task was to "sensitize" the seminaries, the scholasticates, the religious communities and the various ecclesiastical groups, in order to stimulate ecumenical vocations. And so in 1945, with the help and advice of Abbé Couturier, I began to found the "Châtelard Days", for the ecumenical training of priests. This very modest undertaking was, I believe, the first of its kind: it was not imitated till fifteen years later, when ecumenism came to the fore in the perspective of the Council. But by then the "Châtelard Days" had changed their level and were reserved for specialists in more advanced researches, linked with the interdenominational conversations at Dombes. I am glad to pay homage here to the loyalty of the Châtelard team, and especially to the devotion of Fr Michalon, P.S.S., who was able to secure such excellent participants for our sessions.

Up to 1945 my experience was limited to one sort of dialogue, with Protestants of the French kind, and to some relations with Anglicanism. From 1948, being now freed from all other work, I was able to accept invitations which came to me from abroad, and I can never express how much I owe to these contacts with the different Christian Churches. Thus I travelled about Switzerland, England (very discreetly), Denmark, Norway, Finland, Germany, Morocco, Tunisia, Egypt, the Near East through and through, North America and Mexico. Every visit certainly had its history, produced a long chain of friendships, and resulted in unsuspected cares and problems. Is there any better way of traversing the whole ecumenical field? There is one other way, at any rate, and that is a visit to the Institute at Bossey. Now Bossey—first the Institute of the founder, Prof. H. Kraemer, and then that of Dr H. H. Wolf—has been and still is a field of experience for me which gives me much, and to which, under God, I have given something. The University centre of Bossey brings together, in its winter Week, students and professors from the chief denominations; and so all workers in the ecumenical cause—and especially the priests—ought to make a point of spending a period there, for their own instruction.

But the post-war years were no less productive of troubles. The reactions of the Roman Curia, when it found itself again in normal relations with the rest of the world, was one of irritation at the work of doctrinal and pastoral research to which the French theologians, and especially the ecumenists, had devoted themselves. The term "false irenicism" was put in circulation: an ambiguous term which anyone can abuse in order to denounce and thwart a generous enterprise: and it is well known that "delation"—that wretched process unhappily favoured by Canon Law, with no risk to the delator—has every chance of gaining its ends. Rome was inundated with denunciations against the French. We lived under a rule of fear. But in spite of the obstacles (perhaps also from a reflex of solidarity), a consensus of the highest significance could be observed between the French-speaking ecumenists, both those at the centres—Chevetogne, Istina, Lyons—and those like myself who worked in solitude. These specialists knew each other, visited and consulted together, almost it could be said that they thrilled to the same chord. It was what the revered Dom Lambert Beauduin, our forebear, used to call, with his smiling good-humour, "holding *our* ideas". The separated brethren gave their confidence to the French ecumenists, and Dr Visser 't Hooft did not spare his praises for their comprehensive intelligence.

Since I have mentioned Dom Lambert, I am happy to add that he constantly supported me in my difficulties with his advice, encouragement and fatherly solicitude. During his long exile from the monastery he had founded, he lavishly sowed the seeds of unity in France and Belgium, and from this point of view alone his trials were extremely valuable. After twenty years of exile he returned to his sons, to prepare for death. His last words to me, like those of Abbé Couturier, are a memory which never ceases to move me, recalling the blessing of the peacemakers; when they have passed through their trial of persecution they are called "sons of God", and theirs is the kingdom of heaven.

Abbé Couturier died on 24 March 1953, five years before Dom Bauduin, who hailed the Promised Land from afar. As at the death of my mother, I had the feeling that I was walking alone for the first time. Having collected my master's legacy, I wrote his life with love, and then, in a symposium called *Introduction à l'Oecuménisme*, I tried to communicate my now lengthy experience. I was rewarded beyond all my expectations: these two books have been my ambassadors on the long journeys of these latter years and I attribute their wide circulation, not indeed to any merit of theirs, but to the inspiration which dominated them. Everywhere, wherever I am welcomed for ecumenical conferences, I meet the Abbé's peaceful countenance depicted on the crimson cover of the "Église vivante" edition, his eyes looking at me, as once in the little room at the Collège des Chartreux.

But still the enemy is awake. When all seems to be going well, when doors are opening and blessings abound, the insidious attack is launched, denunciations, threats . . . the devilish trap is sprung, and from that moment you are alone, irremediably; your defenders have fled. To suffer *from* the Church when you have given your life *for* her: that too is an experience. It sometimes happens that through the silence one discovers something: the wretchedness of the judicial proceedings, the poverty of the inquiry, the inanity of the criticisms, which, baffled in an *impasse*, end by giving up. *Calca et transi!*

But then at last the dawn broke. On that 25 January 1959, when the Week of Unity was ending, came the promulgation of the Second Vatican Council, and the history of the Church took a new turn. On that day I realized indeed that "Precious in the sight of the Lord is the death of his saints", and that their prayer is victorious. John XXIII is "a man sent from God": in four years he initiates a Gospel epic in the simplicity, candour and purity of the Beatitudes: he gives the Church the "green light" to exchange the sterile stage of monologue with herself for that of dialogue with all the Christian brothers and with the world. Then Paul VI, barely elected, takes up the torch. At the opening of the second session of the Council, before the observers, who can scarcely believe their ears, he solemnly pronounces the Church's *mea culpa* in the matter of the divisions of Christians—a preface which authorizes all their hopes. What does it mean, in fact? Precisely this, that the master-ideas for which the good workers of ecumenism had toiled, fought and suffered for thirty years are those of the schema *De Oecumenismo*, emanating from the Secretariat for Unity. These ideas have proved themselves; they open the dialogue. On the contrary, the doctrinal schemas of scholastic style presented to the first session, which wanted to impose the *status quo*, and even to raise to the level of the extraordinary magisterium statements which would have still further stiffened the Counter-Reformation positions, these schemata (the origin of which we need not recall) were ruthlessly thrown out by a large majority of the Council: for four centuries it had been plain that a presentation of that sort blocked dialogue. Is there not an amazing phenomenon in this sudden change of perspective? But the ecumenical mind, attentive to the movement of the Spirit in all parts of the Christian world, was nonetheless astonished. Its "antennae" had warned it for a long time that the Cathedral of Unity of all men is being built, every man bringing to it his little stone, sometimes at the cost of a whole life, for the marvel cannot be too dearly bought. And when the labourer has placed his little stone, he will lie down in the crypt on the day fixed by the Architect, remembering the verse which Söderblom had inscribed on his tomb in the choir of Uppsala Cathedral:

> When you have done all that is commanded you, say, "We are unworthy servants; we have only done what was our duty" (Luke 17. 10).

[This contribution was translated by P. J. Hepburne-Scott.]

Lukas Vischer

Pastor Lukas Vischer belongs to the Reformed Church at Schaffhausen. He was born in Basle in 1926 and studied at Basle and Oxford Universities. At present he is secretary of the Faith and Order Section of the World Council of Churches.

IS UNITY AN IDOL?

Every year, in numerous Churches separated one from another, Christians begin once again to intercede for unity. The week of prayer for Christian unity is spreading more and more. It was introduced in 1963 into a great number of new Churches and countries and one can state now, without any exaggeration, that it is tending more and more to constitute a link between members of the Christian body. In all parts of the world, during these few days, Orthodox, Roman Catholic and Evangelical Christians stand before God and pray that unity in Christ may be manifested more clearly among them.

Does not this fact constitute an effective promise? Is it not already a preliminary achievement of unity that it should be thus possible for us to unite in prayer, in spite of our differences? It is not a purely natural phenomenon that we should be able to pray together for unity. Our division is so profound that it reaches to our respective conceptions of unity. Even when we all say "unity" this word does not designate the same reality for each of us. And yet prayer permits us to cross even that barrier. In our prayers, we in fact address ourselves to Christ, the source of all real unity, and we present ourselves before God with empty hands waiting for him to fill them afresh. Do not those empty hands exactly express our profound unity?

But does this community of prayer impel us to progress? Can we really say that the unity to which Christ called his disciples is being more and more realized among us? It is necessary to ask this question urgently, for the mere fact of having prayed together does not prove that we are growing in unity. It may be that prayer for unity is becoming a substitute for unity in the true sense of the word. We meet together in union every year, but are we making progress? We are preoccupied with problems concerning unity, but do we subsequently allow ourselves to be moved to action? The week of prayer could become an annual prostration before an idol of unity, a pious gesture with no real bearing on the life of the Church. This danger is all the greater because everyone nowadays is talking of the need for greater unity and because this subject is frequently under discussion.

How can we guard against this inner danger? First and foremost, by truly addressing ourselves to the *Master* of unity in our prayers. It is only by coming closer to him ourselves that we shall come closer to each other. Christ's words "Seek ye first the kingdom of God and his justice and all the rest shall be added to you" can also be applied to the question of unity. The end is the Lordship of Christ and not unity in itself. Wherever Christ begins truly to reign, there results a unity through which men can become signs of God's grace in the world. But as soon as unity is taken for an object in itself, without being attached to him, our efforts lead to nothing. We may exchange excellent conversations, incessantly deepen our awareness of the problems of unity, and acquire in time an extensive knowledge of the whole body of Christianity with all its currents and all its traditions. But at the moment when the heart should appear, the wall will rear up before us as high as ever—the complications of secular history and, above all, the weight of what we take to be immutable data.

At present, the way of unity does not yet appear to us in a perfectly clear light. We know that Christ desires the unity of his disciples. The task before us appears obvious. But when we consider the contradictions that divide us, it is immediately apparent that, humanly speaking, they are irreconcilable. How could they ever arrive at any unity? So it is not surprising to discover a certain attitude of resignation in those who devote themselves intensely to the problems of unity. Are we not working at a task, noble indeed, but impossible of achievement? How could that which is notoriously opposed become one? Would not that mean that someone would have to renounce the truth? Here we touch on the fundamental difficulty in which divided Christianity is floundering. We are perfectly aware of the fact that Christ wishes us to be united, but it is impossible for us to abandon the truth. How can this obstacle be surmounted? Obviously it is not possible to remove it by facile solutions. Our responsibility with regard to the truth is too great. Neither can we fondly imagine that it is the duty of "the other" to renounce the truth which he reserves and that we can remain what we are. We all have a deep-seated need to remain as we are, or at least to stay in line with what we have always been, and this is why we often defend a truth not so much because nothing can shake its hold on us as because we need it in order not to lose continuity with the past. The darkness through which the path to unity leads frightens us; the uncertain and the unknown make us shrink back and we often need the "truth" to protect us from them. Is it not important to remind ourselves here who our Shepherd is, who it is who goes before us on this path? The Shepherd is recognizable by this sign, that he rose from the dead. That is why we cannot accomplish his will if we are content to cling to what constitutes our security. We cannot go forward unless we follow him, even if this seems to demand self-renunciation in a darkness filled with uncertainty. For all of us, the way of unity is a path that leads to resurrection through death. Many things which we love, which are familiar to us and which it seems impossible to us to renounce must die in order to give place to his will. What Christ demands of us is always so new that we have to leave behind us what we thought we possessed in order to be ready together to welcome the future he offers us. May the week of prayer help us to let ourselves be impregnated afresh by this truth.

[This contribution was translated by Antonia White.]